Recasting Science

Recasting Science

Consensual Procedures in Public Policy Making

Connie P. Ozawa

Westview Press
BOULDER • SAN FRANCISCO • OXFORD

This Westview softcover edition is printed on acid-free paper and bound in library-quality, coated covers that carry the highest rating of the National Association of State Textbook Administrators, in consultation with the Association of American Publishers and the Book Manufacturers' Institute.

All rights reserved. No part of this publication may be reproduced or transmitted in any form or by any means, electronic or mechanical, including photocopy, recording, or any information storage and retrieval system, without permission in writing from the publisher.

Copyright © 1991 by Westview Press, Inc.

Published in 1991 in the United States of America by Westview Press, Inc., 5500 Central Avenue, Boulder, Colorado 80301, and in the United Kingdom by Westview Press, 36 Lonsdale Road, Summertown, Oxford OX2 7EW

Library of Congress Cataloging-in-Publication Data
Ozawa, Connie P.
  Recasting science : consensual procedures in public policy making / Connie P. Ozawa.
    p. cm.
  Includes bibliographical references and index.
  ISBN 0-8133-7961-X
  1. Policy sciences. 2. Scientists in government. I. Title.
H97.093 1991
320'.6—dc20   90-21792
                                                                                 CIP

Printed and bound in the United States of America

∞   The paper used in this publication meets the requirements of the American National Standard for Permanence of Paper for Printed Library Materials Z39.48-1984.

10   9   8   7   6   5   4   3   2   1

For Daniel
and Jacqueline

Contents

List of Tables and Figures	ix
Preface	xi
Acknowledgments	xiii

1 Political Uses of Science in Public Decision Making   1

Science in Public Debates, 1
Science as a Mechanism of Accountability, 4
Authority and the "Nature" of Science, 5
Science as a Weapon: Legitimation and Persuasion, 8
The Ascent of Science in Policy Making, 9
Notes, 12

2 The Dynamics of Advocacy Science   13

Public Decision Making Institutions, 13
Methods for Handling Scientific Information, 28
Structuring the Use of Science and Its Consequences, 32
Summary, 41
Notes, 42

3 Consensus-Based Approaches to Handling Science   45

Foundations for Change, 45
Three Procedures for Science-Intensive Decision Making, 51
Restructuring the Use of Science, 72
Notes, 76

4 Power Dynamics in Consensual Procedures   79

Mapping the Battlefield: Science in Four Phases
  of Decision Making, 80
Shifting Winds of Power? 87
Consequences for Power, 96
Notes, 102

5 Prospects for Change   105

   Miscast Roles for Science in Public Decision Making, 105
   Recasting Science Through Consensus-Based Procedures, 107
   Viability of Consensus-Based Procedures, 112
   Should We Use Consensual Procedures? 122
   Notes, 126

Appendix 1   127
Appendix 2   129
Bibliography   131
Index   139

Tables and Figures

Tables

5.1 Distinctive features of three consensus-based procedures   108

5.2 Major advantages and disadvantages of conventional and consensus-based procedures for policy actors by major category   114

Figures

2.1 Communication flows in conventional information-eliciting procedures   29

2.2 Communication flows in conventional dispute resolution procedures   30

Preface

Science has been ubiquitous in public decision making in the United States in the 1980s and promises to serve no less a role in the decade and new century ahead. Government actions are justified on the basis of scientific evidence in an overwhelming array of issue areas. Legislating health warnings on cigarette packaging in the 1960s, banning the use of cyclamates, phasing down the lead content of gasoline in the 1970s, and denying construction permits for projects in ecologically sensitive locations are just a few of the multitudinous ways that our public agencies at various levels of government have availed of scientific expertise to assist in the making of public policy throughout the recent decades. Relying on science to make decisions or to resolve disputes is a political tactic, however, and one that threatens to subvert democratic decision making.

Conventional decision making processes cast science into a "conquer or perish" role. Science is held up not as one standard (among many) by which to fashion wise policy options but rather as a weapon wielded by contending stakeholders endeavoring to defeat alternatives they find less desirable. Groups advocating certain policy alternatives marshal out corroborating scientific information and analysis or, more pointedly, arguments or alternative theories that question the soundness of competing policy options. Decision makers, or those responsible for orchestrating the public decision making process, respond by initiating a variety of procedures ostensibly designed to resolve technical disagreements and either establish the superiority of one policy option over others (because of its consistency with the "correct" understanding of technical parameters) or establish the technical constraints within which political claims can be subsequently settled. In neither case is the political nature of scientific argument itself considered.

This book explores the use of science in public decision making, argues that conventional decision making procedures create conditions conducive to unconstructive approaches toward handling scientific information, and suggests that consensus-based procedures offer opportunities for reconciling the political values in science with the more overt political contests seething beneath the surface of public decisions. The discussion is organized around three examples of public decision making, first drawing hypothetical scenarios of conventional decision making and then contrasting these with conventional decision making supplemented by consensus-based procedures. Chapter 2, which includes the hypothetical scenarios, contains an inventory and critique of conventional methods for handling scientific information and disputes. In Chapter 3, the same decision making cases are used to describe three different, actual consensus-based procedures. The analysis considers how these consensus-based procedures measure up against the criticisms of conventional methods and how the role of science is recast.

Changes in decision making processes are not without a redistribution of bias, however. Whether through simple familiarity with the procedures or because of more fixed political economic relationships, some groups are favored by the more prevalent, conventional decision making procedures. Changes in convention may cause such groups to lose their edge, however momentarily. Hence, Chapter 4 explores some of the changes in the dynamics of influence that occurred in the cases studied and suggests additional ways that the balance of "power" may change by the augmentation of conventional decision making with consensus-based procedures.

Finally, the advantages and disadvantages of consensus-based procedures are not identical for various stakeholding parties in decisions relying heavily on scientific expertise and information. Moreover, the relative attractiveness of consensus-based procedures compared with the conventional decision making process is likely to vary according to a number of factors unique to any given situation. In the concluding chapter, we consider what these factors are and how stakeholding groups can assess the desirability and political wisdom of participating in a consensus-based procedure.

A discussion of science in public decision making would not be complete without first looking at the history of science in the public decision making institutions. Hence, we begin this discourse in Chapter 1 with a review of the ascent of science and the multiple roles it has played in decision making in the United States.

Connie P. Ozawa

Acknowledgments

Any major project is the work of many, many persons, most of whose contributions pass unrecognized. Although this book formally represents research conducted during my doctoral studies, many of the concerns and ideas explored and extended in this manuscript were presented to me long before the initiation of this project. Consequently, I owe thanks to a lengthy list of persons and situations that helped to direct my curiosity, which eventually led to this inquiry.

In these lines, however, I wish to extend special appreciation to individuals and organizations who provided exceptional support, encouragement, and intellectual guidance in the more concrete phases of this project. I thank Larry Susskind for his commitment to procedural innovations in public decision making and his relentless energy, which continues to inspire so many of us. I am grateful to Deborah Stone and Larry Bacow for helping me to set my questions within a larger policy framework, Harvey Brooks for his helpful insights about the roles of experts, and Deborah Kolb and Michael Wheeler for their help in clarifying and organizing some of the arguments contained in this book.

I would also like to acknowledge the various participants and observers of the cases who tirelessly explained many, many details through lengthy and sometimes multiple conversations. Their openness, interest, and enthusiasm in discussing their experiences were contagious. In particular, I thank Marc David Block at the New York Academy of Sciences, Robert Doherty, Chris Kirtz of the Environmental Protection Agency, and Steve Konkel for sharing documents, interpretations, and insights; conversations with each helped me to understand more clearly what issues were of greatest concern to me.

The National Institute for Dispute Resolution in Washington, D.C., and the Center for Environmental Management at Tufts University provided essential support through research grants. I am grateful to Rob Hollister for facilitating these awards. My coworkers at the Program on Negotiation, Harvard Law School, made my working environment pleasant, egged me on, rescued me during panic-stricken moments, and helped to furnish the finishing touches on this manuscript. Thanks especially to Bill Breslin and Denis Achacoso.

Finally, I am indebted to my parents, family, and friends who provided me the emotional stability so necessary for forward movement. I give special thanks to Gerry for the intellectual exercises his questions have posed for me over the years, for the hours and hours he spent helping put this manuscript into its final form, and, most especially, for his patience, humor, and companionship throughout this enterprise.

C.P.O.

1

Political Uses of Science in Public Decision Making

Science in Public Debates

When public health advocates brought their indictment against cigarettes to the steps of Capitol Hill in the 1960s, they faced a formidable opponent. The economically wealthy, well-organized, and extensive tobacco defense network included paid representatives of tobacco growers, cigarette manufacturers, and marketing organizations; congresspersons from tobacco growing regions; prominent members of four congressional subcommittees that handle tobacco legislation and appropriations; and officials at the Department of Agriculture involved with tobacco programs. Although many health professionals believed that cigarette smoking caused ill-health as early as the turn of the century, it was not until the early 1950s that public health advocates had in hand results from large-scale epidemiological studies indicating a strong association between smoking and lung cancer. Recognizing the potential potency of research findings linking cigarette smoking and disease, the tobacco industry responded quickly to preliminary findings by establishing the Tobacco Industry Research Committee (now called the Council for Tobacco Research-U.S.A.) (Fritschler).

What ensued was a lengthy debate over the scientific evidence proving a causal link between cigarette smoking and disease. The tobacco industry continually attacked the use of statistical evidence by anti-smoking advocates. The epidemiological studies showed correlations between cigarette smoking and the incidence of ill-health, but could not prove causality. The industry argued, for example, that variables uncontrolled in the study, such as lifestyle patterns, genetic traits, and environmental factors might have a stronger causal relationship with disease than cigarette smoking. In fact, two contrasting theories to explain the association between cigarette smoking and lung cancer were promoted: one suggested a causal link and the other attributed both the behavior and disease to the genetic composition of individuals (in other words, that a genetic factor is responsible for both an individual's predisposition to smoking and susceptibility to develop cancer). Ultimately, the genetic theory proved to be less persuasive to public officials and they elected to take regulatory action.

Congressional action requiring a health warning on each package of cigarettes was only one victory in a continuing war between public health advocates and pro-smoking interests. The industry committed heavily to its defense. From 1954-1980, the Council for Tobacco Research awarded 744 grants investing $64 million in research by 413 scientists at 258 hospitals, laboratories, research institutions, and medical schools. An additional $15 million was contributed to the American Medical Association Education and Research Foundation, which then did not actively support the anti-smoking campaign, by the six major cigarette producers to support research on tobacco and health between 1964-1973 (Fritschler).[1]

The 1987 congressional debate over banning cigarette smoking on all air flights of two hours or less duration revived familiar arguments about the scientific basis of public policy to curtail tobacco use. For example, a spokesperson for the Tobacco Institute, Inc.,[2] argued on national television that the three existing studies conducted on airlines in-flight do not show that the level of exposure to cigarette smoke experienced by non-smokers is hazardous to their health (Merryman). Once again, the tobacco defenders drew on its arsenal of scientific studies to deflect growing public concern about the detrimental health effects of the industry's products.

When the United States Environmental Protection Agency (EPA) proposed regulations in early 1972 to reduce the amount of lead additives in gasoline, the Ethyl Corporation began a vigorous and persistent attack on the factual basis of EPA's decision. The Ethyl Corporation challenged whether reducing the amount of lead in gasoline would eliminate the health hazard of airborne lead to the extent suggested by one of the major EPA source documents (Collingridge). Ethyl also contested EPA's assertion that the catalytic converter, a technology that required lead-free fuel, was the only automobile air pollution control system that would be operational by 1975. Later rounds of the debate focussed more precisely on specific claims made by EPA in regard to identifying susceptible populations, the relative contributions of other sources of lead in blood, assessment of "acceptable" blood lead levels, and the correlation between air lead concentrations and blood lead levels. Each claim made by EPA to support a phased-down reduction of lead in gasoline was countered by the Ethyl Corporation.

The record of the resultant lawsuit alone numbered more than 10,000 pages (*Ethyl Corporation v. EPA*). Much of the argumentation revolved on the scientific and technical premises of the Agency's decision to regulate lead additives in gasoline. As the presiding District Court noted, the evidence was far from conclusive and, "[Scientific] evidence may be isolated that supports virtually any inference one might care to draw" (*Ethyl Corporation v. EPA*). Again, the scientific basis of the decision was an integral part of the public debate, and each side of the eventual lawsuit invested considerable resources to substantiate its position with appropriate scientific and technical evidence.

When the state of New York and the city of New York jointly proposed to reconstruct the West Side Highway in lower Manhattan in what proponents described as a "mechanism for stimulating jobs, investment; an innovative urban design that will revitalize Manhattan's West Side," project opponents quickly organized to block it (Wanderstock: 77). Although opponents mobilized around a list of issues including the project's ability to address its primary objective, transportation, they pegged their first courtroom attack on the adequacy of the draft Environmental Impact Statement (EIS) rendered in 1974 in accordance with the National Environmental Policy Act (NEPA). Subsequent lawsuits contested the final EIS claim concerning an area of the Hudson River targeted for landfill. The EIS, issued in January 1977, stated that this "interpier area" was incapable of supporting significant aquatic life. After prodding by the EPA, however, the Westway Project conducted a 13-month study that revealed this water area supported 22 species of fish. The eventual demise of the Westway Project can be attributed in large part to the project's delay, but the final death blow was struck by the scientific studies that indicated the extent of the project's likely environmental impacts, particularly with regard to the aquatic ecosystem.

These cases are only three examples of a recurring trend in public decision making in the United States. In actions ranging from congressional law making and federal administrative rulemaking to local, site-specific construction projects, lengthy reviews and debates over scientific and technical information are commonplace. In the legislature, scientific evidence is often cited as a compelling reason for formulation of public policy. Indeed, congressional actions that ultimately resulted in the requirement for a health warning on cigarette packaging were a response, albeit indirect, to a 1964 report by the Surgeon General, that, in turn, was a reaction to surmounting scientific evidence on both sides of the Atlantic linking cigarette smoking to ill-health. The EPA's action to reduce airborne lead was directed by the 1970 Clean Air Act (CAA) Amendments. The EPA was explicitly instructed, under Section 108, to prepare a criteria document for each pollutant that "endangers the public health" and, under Section 109, to establish ambient air quality standards for such pollutants necessary to protect the public health and welfare. In the West Side Highway controversy, the technical assessment of predicted environmental damage, required by the National

Environmental Policy Act, proved pivotal in the decision to abandon the project.

Science as a Mechanism of Accountability

Scientific knowledge did not always play such a prominent role in public decision making. Prior to the administration of Franklin D. Roosevelt, scientific and technical analysis and argument were consulted explicitly by government decision makers only sporadically (and then mostly during wartime) (Lakoff; Mullins; West). The creation of the New Deal agencies, however, signalled the beginning of an era of delegated decision making, with important consequences for the use of science and technical expertise in public decisions (Lowi; West). Indeed, part of the rationale for the establishment of independent government agencies was the more specialized knowledge in relevant technical areas that agency personnel were expected to contribute.

Almost as soon as the agencies were established, Congress acted to ensure a method of accountability. The Administrative Procedures Act (APA) of 1946 was a congressional response to concern about the discretionary powers of administrative agencies and independent commissions, which were insulated from both the electorate and Congress. The APA prescribes rulemaking procedures for agency decision making, and requires that formal rulemaking be based "on the record" (West). The "record" includes transcripts of testimony and exhibits, findings and conclusions, exceptions to the decision, and supporting reasons for the exceptions or proposed findings or conclusions (Barry and Whitcomb). As agencies began to deal increasingly with issues concerning public health, new technology, and the environment, the pressure to demonstrate a rational basis for decisions led decision makers to more carefully attend to the consistency of their decisions with the findings of pertinent scientific and technical studies and analysis.

More recently, legislators have moved to broaden the range of agency decision making falling under the umbrella of public scrutiny. In some cases, statutes, such as the Occupational Safety and Health Act (OSHA), the Toxic Substances Control Act (TSCA), and the Consumer Protection and Safety Act (CPSA), contain "hybrid" rulemaking procedures, requiring that even "informal rulemaking" similarly be based "on the record." In other cases, directives for scientific analysis is explicitly mandated in congressional legislation. The Clean Air Act, for example, instructs EPA to issue air quality criteria for air pollutants that "accurately reflect the latest scientific knowledge useful in indicating the kind and extent of all identifiable effects on public health and welfare" (Clean Air Act).

Finally, more expansive laws, such as the National Environmental Policy Act (NEPA) of 1969, have brought the importance of scientific and technical factors into the forefront of decision making on a wider array of issues. NEPA, which has been duplicated in modified form by many state governments, mandates that all decisions on actions availing of federal funds give full consideration to possible adverse environmental consequences of the proposed actions. Projects ranging from construction of a backyard toolshed to off-shore oil leasing now may require an appraisal of the environmental impact.

The proliferation of decision making prescriptions in legislation, along with sunshine laws and the Freedom of Information Act, prompted the development of a number of quasi-technical decision aids, including cost-benefit analysis and its more recent derivative, risk-benefit analysis. One important feature of such analytical aids is their quantitative nature. Not only do they help decision makers distinguish between possible decision alternatives, the decision maker and others can refer back to these methods to retrace their decision making calculus. In theory, these analytical aids are intended to add clarity to the decision making process, disclosing to the public the rationale behind particular decisions. (In fact, these technical aids have frequently become part of the substance of challenges to decisions.)

Congressional directives to administrative decision makers to consult the growing bodies of scientific knowledge were initially intended to ensure a certain accountability among executive office appointees. Specifically, these procedural prescriptions were seen as some assurance that decisions were not simply the product of narrow political interests, raw political ambition, or personal whim. Even under this model, however, the political neutrality of decisions was limited, since more than one policy alternative may be consistent with any given set of circumstances. Nonetheless, the discretionary arm of executive agencies was believed to be critically restrained by these legislative decision making prescriptions.

Authority and the "Nature" of Science

Astute elected officials soon recognized a second benefit from the use of scientific and technical analysis in decision making. In addition to helping to keep a check on the discretionary powers of administrative agencies, scientific and technical analysis could be advantageous to their own policy making efforts. In 1957, the President's Science Advisory Committee was established to counsel the Executive Officer on the technical merits and consequences of specific programs (Fischer). The U.S. Congress set up the Office of Technology Assessment (OTA) in 1972 to provide legislators advice on technical and scientific aspects of important issues, as well as to study the social, economic, and political impacts of new technological developments. Although information about technologies and the scientific parameters of particular situations is important in itself to decision making, the political punch of boasting that choices are consistent with "what the experts say" was not long overlooked.

In the economic and cultural context of the 20th-century United States and, indeed, in much of the industrialized world, science serves as a source of authority. This authority is intimately linked to a popularly conceived notion of the scientific enterprise that is based on a certain ideal of science. According to this ideal, science is a process that yields an objective, rational, politically neutral body of knowledge that presents a single, coherent understanding of reality. Consequently, decisions shown to be consistent with scientific knowledge command acceptance. After all, Mother Nature is not to be crossed. Actions that are congruent with her laws and design are wiser, it is believed, than alternatives whose compatibility is unknown or uncharted.

A principal feature in the popular understanding of the scientific enterprise is its strict methodological prescriptions. According to the dominant philosophy of science through the 1960s, known as logical positivist empiricism, the primary test of truth is the replicability of experimental findings. Hiskes and Hiskes write that logical positivist empiricism assumes that

1. data obtained through careful experiment and observation are objective,
2. there is one universally valid logic for science, and
3. through rigorous application of logic to data, science gradually makes progress toward the ancient Greek ideal of *theoria* (Hiskes and Hiskes: 10–11).

According to the logical positivist empiricist view, data are incontrovertible and unchanging. Any rational person observing the same event would report identical observations. The recording of data eventually leads to the development of theory that integrates abstract concepts and generalizable principles to explain diverse phenomena. Logic is linear and one-directional. In short, this view implies that the products of work undertaken through the scientific method are absolute and without ambiguity.

The characterization of science as a dispassionate activity, (that is, one that does not depend on the views of the individual scientist), has deep roots. Francis Bacon was instrumental in crystallizing this view as far back as the 1500s (Lakoff). As the formal architect of the modern method of scientific inquiry, (which prescribes the setting and testing of hypotheses as the means of establishing fact), he sought to outline a way of accumulating knowledge about the physical world that was free of theologically-based distortion and founded on the observation of reality rather than imagination or fancy. Moreover, to depict science in a manner that would be palatable to the then powerful religious establishment, Bacon carefully delineated the territory of science and claimed that the science of nature "is studiously indifferent to good and evil" (Lakoff: 9).

Bacon (and others) advocated this image of science during a period in which intense disputes over critical theological and philosophical issues were disrupting English society as well as life on the European continent (Ben-David). The growing popularity of the Baconian view at that time is attributable to the widely shared belief that a consensus on procedures is neutral with respect to religion or politics. What later became known as "the scientific method" represented a way for intellectual thought to progress in England amidst the country's civil revolution. Most scientists concurred with this apolitical image of science. One historian writes,

> One of the often-mentioned features of the prehistory of the Royal Society [an organization of scientists in Britain] is that the participants at the informal meetings of the circle from which the society emerged agreed not to discuss matters of religion or politics but to restrict themselves dispassionately to the neutral field of science (Ben-David: 72).

In more recent years, scientists and their spokespersons have aggressively fought to reaffirm and protect the image of a neutral science. Proponents of financial support for scientific research by the federal government have argued that the scientific community is and ought to be allowed to remain autonomous. The scientific community has been called a "priesthood" (Lapp), an "estate" (Price), and a "republic" (Polanyi) and scientists, accordingly, have been described as "objective," "disinterested," "uncorruptible," and "impartial" (Wood). Once again, uniform standards of validating fact and the self-imposed discipline of the scientific method are offered as guarantees that science is a depersonalized and selfless quest for truth on behalf of the "common good."

Contemporary scientists, wittingly or not, reinforce the image of a neutral science when testifying on specific public policy issues by claiming to distinguish between their "professional" and their "personal" views. In the debate over the regulation of chlorofluoromethanes (CFMs), for example, one scientist appearing before a Senate committee in 1975 stated,

> I should point out that the measurements that I am involved in are crucial to the question [of banning aerosol sprays] and I would like to remain neutral on such a question as you ask until I satisfy myself of the results of those measurements. That is from a scientific point of view. From the personal point of view, I feel very strongly about the issue of protecting the very delicate ozone photochemistry, and from that point of view I would urge on the basis of the data and calculations already available that action be taken (Brooks: 207).

The presumption underlying the distinction between a "scientific point of view" and a "personal point of view" is that one is devoid of value intervention while the other is not.

As a result of the sharp demarcation between politics and science, science supporters have frequently and openly defended the central, advisory role they believe scientists ought to play in policy making (Burger; Crandall and Lave). They lament that scientific advice is often ignored or sacrificed for the sake of "democratic decision making" and that the public is not interested in advice that is objective and analytical (Burger). In a full closing of the circle, so to speak, the individual scientist who conducts scientific study is portrayed as neutral when reporting on work conducted in accordance with the rigid structure of the scientific method. And, the image of a neutral science has been extended to the belief that scientific work even in the context of public policy debates is "studiously indifferent" not only to good and evil, but also to who wins and who loses.

In Baconian England, science competed with religion and the monarchy as a way of interpreting and explaining the world and making decisions about future actions. Gradually, science proponents created an image of science, not unaided by incredible technological feats, that engendered among the public a trust in the ability of the scientific method to attain the highest level of understanding the natural world that society had ever known. Full acceptance of science as a way of knowing was achieved when "instead of needing justification from other more fundamental values, science became a source and a standard of legitimacy" (Greenfield: 122).

Science as a Weapon: Legitimation and Persuasion

From the authority invested in a science viewed as politically neutral, it was a small step to exploit science as a political tool. Over the years, science has come to play multiple roles in decision making. First and foremost, scientific knowledge can be viewed as critical to evaluating the wisdom of decisions, since an action that conflicts with what is understood about the natural world may be considered foolish and undesirable. Second, as noted earlier in this chapter, consistency with scientific knowledge can be seen as a check, albeit partial, on discretionary decision making power. A third and no less prevalent use (not unrelated to the first two) has evolved, however, arising with the widespread acceptance of the logical positivist empiricist view of science and the creation of institutional frameworks that require reference to scientific knowledge. As many writers have observed, science is looked upon as a source of authority for justifying decisions and persuading competing elements of the polity of the legitimacy of one alternative over others (Dickson; Majone; Nelkin and Pollack). Like religion and the rule of the monarchy prior to the Age of Enlightenment, science is invoked in twentieth century decision making as a primary source of legitimacy to gain political support:

> By invoking the authoritative canons of scientific reasoning and method, public authorities and others having a stake in technical issues seek to demonstrate the rationality of their position and thereby gain political support and acceptance (Brickman: 108).

In other words, rather than to ensure wise decisions or to demonstrate a sort of accountability, scientific arguments are frequently marshalled out in controversial cases for strategic purposes by decision makers or others trying to influence decisions. For example, decision makers fearful of the consequences of politically unpopular decisions seek refuge in scientific and technical arguments indicating the "soundness" of their decisions. As one writer has noted with regard to policies for protecting health and the environment, "turning the job of defining adequate standards over to 'experts' relieves congressmen of the burden of resolving difficult controversies" (Melnick: 251). Administrative agencies aware of the possibility of lawsuits challenging their decisions and the scope of judicial review fortify their decisions with appropriate scientific or technical support.

The power of scientific argument to legitimize the actions of decision makers also provides a means for challenging a decision, however. Nelkin has written that "access to knowledge and the resulting ability to question the data used to legitimize decisions is an essential basis of power and influence" (Nelkin, 1980: 16). Groups unhappy with a decision, or expected decision, amass scientific evidence to contradict the decision's scientific basis and thereby undermine its legitimacy, as did the Ethyl Corporation in their suit against the EPA on airborne lead and the Tobacco Institute in the debate leading to anti-smoking legislation.

Moreover, the use of scientific arguments is not always free of deception. Sometimes such groups tend to exaggerate their arguments in order to garner greater political support (Douglas and Wildavsky). Industry has been observed to systematically underestimate health risks (Marcus). In short, a major use of science in public decision making in the United States is as a weapon wielded by contending interest groups.

The Ascent of Science in Policy Making

It is clear that science is widely accepted as a desirable factor in public decision making, but how has scientific and technical expertise come to play such a prominent role in contentious debates over public decisions? A number of speculations have been suggested.[3] On one dimension, advances in technology have had the dual effect of enhancing the ability to detect smaller and smaller increments of change and at the same time creating new sources of potential offenders. That is, instruments and testing procedures now allow researchers to detect contamination of air or water at concentrations of "parts per billion," or even "parts per trillion," in some cases, whereas earlier, "parts per million" was the limit. Concurrently, human activities have escalated and developed in a direction that creates undesirable environmental impacts. One writer argued that,

> pollution is a direct consequence of the anti-ecological nature of a laissez-faire technology not properly assessed and controlled, and designed only to reinforce existing political and economic structures (Knelman: 48).

Finally, it can be argued that the cumulative nature of environmental and health impacts required the passage of a certain period of time before change was measurable. Commoner has argued that pollution first widely observed in the 1970s was the result of technological changes that had been occurring since the 1940s (Commoner, 1972). In short, these arguments and others that focus on technologies suggest that because society's awareness of environmental impacts has been heightened, the subject of public decisions is now more technical in nature than in previous times.

More compelling than the shaping of public issues by technological change to explain the use of scientific arguments in contentious decisions, however, are factors that concern the individuals and groups behind these contests. The liberal social and political climate of the 1960s planted an expectation of "rights" among proliferating organized interest groups in the United States (Cigler and Loomis; O'Connor). The population and its elected leaders felt entitled to a certain standard of living. "Clean air" and "navigable, swimmable, and drinkable waters" were viewed as a right, not a privilege. This attitude was reflected in federal legislation that conferred legal standing on the general citizenry to enable "any person" to file a "citizen's suit" against pollution sources to enforce emission standards or against the EPA administrator for failure to carry out provisions of federal environmental legislation (Stewart and Krier: 642).[4] Moreover, the notion of public decision making changed. Beginning with President Johnson's New Society rhetoric about "maximum feasible participation" of those affected in public decisions, both the rhetoric and the reality of governmental decisions now reflect a greater commitment for involving the citizenry (Freedman: 47).

Along with expanded enfranchisement, environmental, community, and consumer groups have also grown more sophisticated. The organization of environmental, community, and consumer groups in the 1960s provided an alternative ideological home for scientists, engineers, lawyers, and other highly trained professionals. Up until then, professionals either aligned with industry or government for research funding. The degree to which university researchers were independent of industry or government agenda is debatable, but certainly the development of environmental, community, and consumer groups provided an outlet for university researchers to enter public debates in a new way (Primack and Von Hippel). Thus, while the potential for general societal conflict increased on several fronts (additional sources of infractions of rights, enhanced means for measuring infractions of rights, a broadening definition of defensible rights, growing opportunities for individuals to express perceptions of violations, and others), scientific and technical expertise in service to ideologically organized interests also expanded.

"The battle of the print-out" and other adversarial uses of scientific work has become more common, then, not merely because of the growth in legal and institutional structures that encourage it, but because of an increasing ability of contending groups to avail of the persuasive power of scientific and technical argumentation. Disputes over scientific or technical elements of public decisions emerge not from computer print-outs or purely scholarly disagreement, but from differing perceptions and valuations of the political, economic, and social consequences of decisions.

Stakeholding groups perceive a peculiar distribution of costs and benefits resulting from a given public decision (Wilson). These costs and benefits, or political interests, may concern individual, material or psychological gains or losses, the precedent-setting value of legal interpretations or interpretations of a particular agency's mandate and philosophy, or public statements on morality. For example, although an investigation would probably also show that even the earliest studies on the relationship of cigarette smoking to human disease arose from a concern for protecting public health, the motivation of the tobacco industry for funding research on smoking and cancer was clear. They acted out of a perception of a threat to their economic interest (should the health warning dissuade people from smoking) and, perhaps, to avert the moral condemnation of the tobacco industry conveyed by a public statement acknowledging the detrimental effect of smoking on public health. The Ethyl Corporation challenged EPA's scientific analyses for similar reasons. When groups become concerned about what they view as adverse impacts on their interests, then they mobilize to support or contest public decisions. Challenges to the scientific and technical basis of public decisions and policy alternatives are launched by these groups for strategic purposes. Disputes arise not from the spontaneous emergence of contradictory scientific evidence but from the mobilization of political interests by individuals and groups holding a stake in those decisions.

If the claims about the nature of science made by logical positivist empiricism held true, the use of science to legitimate decision choices and persuade the polity would not be disturbing. After all, who could argue that scientifically unwise decisions are preferable to scientifically wise ones? Different interest groups may be vying for preferred policies or decisions, but their claims would at least be in the interest of general society if the scientific information on which their positions were formed was, indeed, indisputable.

However, the scientific enterprise rarely achieves the logical positivist empiricist ideal of science. Whereas the objectives of science may be to attain truth, individual scientific undertakings represent only tiny steps toward truth. Knowledge gained through the scientific method is the accumulation of bits and pieces of reality, voluminous but incomplete, and mediated by the collector. Competing versions of scientifically derived "truth" can, and often do, coexist.

The capacity of a broader range of groups to utilize scientific and technical argumentation has caused a dispersion of access to the authoritative power of science. That scientific and technical analysis have become central pillars in challenges to the formulation and determination of controversial decisions in the legislatures and courts as well as in administrative agencies (at the federal, state, and municipal levels) signals a qualitative change in the dynamics of influence over those decisions. Not all groups in society have enjoyed the same gains in access to science and influence. Thus, how scientific and technical information, especially conflicting evidence, is managed in public forums holds tremendous implications for government decisions regarding public resource allocations and the prospects for social justice.

Notes

1. The American Medical Association adopted a resolution acknowledging an association between the incidence of lung cancer and cigarette smoking on June 24, 1965.

2. The Tobacco Institute, Inc., is a lobbying, public relations organization formed in 1958 by fourteen major tobacco producers. The company presidents of these firms sit on the Institute's board of directors.

3. For a discussion about the factors that have led to greater interest in the social control of technology, see Harvey Brooks, "Controlling Technology: Risks, Costs, and Benefits," in *Technology and Politics*, ed. Michael E. Kraft and Norman J. Vig (Durham, N.C.: Duke University Press, 1988), 168–183.

4. See, for example, Section 304(a) of the Clean Air Act. Other federal statutes with similar provisions include the Federal Water Pollution Control Act, the Noise Contol Act of 1972, the Safe Drinking Water Act of 1974, and the Marine Protection Research Sanctuaries Act of 1972.

2

The Dynamics of Advocacy Science

Public Decision Making Institutions

Consider first how public decisions conventionally unfold in the United States. Public decision making in the United States occurs in three general arenas: decision making by elected officials (executives, legislators, city councillors, etc.); administrative decision making; and judicial decision making. Decision making in these arenas at all levels of government (federal, regional, state, or local) frequently requires the consideration of scientific or technical information and analysis. Elected officials often refer to scientific and technical evidence when setting policy on environmental, health, and safety issues (as in the cigarette smoking policy debates), deciding whether to appropriate funds for public projects (as in the New York City waste processing facility controversy, discussed further on), and granting development permits for site-specific projects at the local level (as in the West Side Highway case). Administrative agencies with delegated authority to implement broad policy objectives are often legislatively required to demonstrate that their decisions are supported by appropriate technical documentation. Finally, the courts handle cases steeped in scientific controversy, such as liability suits in science-intensive "toxic tort" cases, and provide legal recourse for challenges to administrative decision making.

When perceived stakes are high among groups sufficiently organized, competent, and resourceful, scientific information on which decisions ostensibly are based often becomes the focus of public debate. That is, groups able to gain access to appropriate expertise and resources understand the strategic value of scientific testimony and use it accordingly, to question, delay and even block the approval and implementation of an undesired decision.

Such strategic orchestration of scientific arguments is conducted especially in cases in which the costs of delaying a decision fall asymmetrically on different parties. Delaying a permit decision on a nuclear power plant, for example, imposes substantial financial expenses on the utility company, but little costs on project opponents. Conversely, postponing the enforcement of regulations to abate pollution saves polluters the monetary burden of pollution control while incrementally degrading air or water quality and public health. In both types of cases, the group profiting by delay can be expected to manipulate scientific arguments to cast doubt on the scientific underpinnings of proposed actions.

Decision making involving highly contentious and technically complex issues is complicated. When one or more parties benefits from postponing a decision and has little incentive to bring the issue to a close, efforts to resolve the dispute will confront sometimes insurmountable obstacles. Parties benefitting from delay will exhaust all legal and political options they can afford before agreeing to a final decision. Years may pass before a final, binding (usually court) decision is rendered.

Occasionally, however, the costs of delaying a decision fall more or less symmetrically on several major parties. In these instances, both proponents and opponents are burdened by the uncertainty of an impending decision, are penalized by indecision, or see clear advantages in a speedy resolution of the dispute. Controversies concerning decisions about a development proposal in the early stages is an example of one type of such cases. A speedy decision is favorable to a developer who may wish to invest his effort and monies on a more probable (though, perhaps, less lucrative) project, if necessary. On the other hand, a neighborhood may prefer a quick decision, even if it is affirmative, in order to begin to organize itself and mobilize sympathy and support from the wider community.

Another example is the approval or disapproval of a new drug. Without a clear decision either way, the sponsoring pharmaceutical company may continue to pour dollars into research directed toward winning approval from the U.S. Food and Drug Administration. Meanwhile, the company may defer the funding of alternative research items, deferring potential benefits from such research as well. While those advocating caution in the use of new drugs may feel confident that approval of a specific new drug is unwarranted, they would probably not be opposed to the conduct of research in other areas by the same pharmaceutical company. A decision either way would free up research dollars for the pharmaceutical firm; an affirmative decision would encourage public health advocates either to step up their challenge or to redirect their efforts toward other areas.

A third example of such cases are cases in which the costs previously fell asymmetrically on the parties, but circumstances changed and the costs to a party initially benefitting from delay increased to the extent that uncertainty is no longer financially or politically bearable. For example, while opposition to a development permit may succeed in delaying the issuing of a necessary permit, the economic and organizational resources needed to sustain a visible public campaign eventually may become depleted. While opponents would prefer a flat denial of the permit application, even an affirmative decision may improve the political resources of the opposing group, by presenting them with a more concrete rallying point to take to the public, or to the courts.

Finally, decision makers themselves may find that continued delay is not desirable. Administrative agencies often operate under time deadlines imposed by legislators or a negotiated lawsuit settlement and failing to make a timely decision may result in default of their duty or violation of an agreement. State-level agencies may face deadlines imposed by federal funding sources. Elected officials may feel compelled to bring some kind of closure to an issue before an election changes the cast of players.

Recognition of the cost of delay in public decision making (economic and political as well as human costs incurred when health- or safety-related regulations are delayed or implementation postponed by challenges to their scientific premises) has spurred interest, investment, and experimentation in ways to integrate scientific and technical information into public decision making. A number of procedures have evolved in our public decision making institutions to address cases like these, in which all parties perceive they have more to gain from a decision than from indecision. These procedures tend to concentrate specifically on facilitating the collection of scientific and technical information and the resolution of scientific disagreement.

In the following sections, three hypothetical, decision making scenarios, which are built around actual cases in which consensus-based procedures were used to supplement conventional decision making procedures, are presented. These hypothetical scenarios are intended to serve three purposes. First, they provide a common conception of the mechanics of conventional legislative, administrative, and judicial decision making. Since actual public decision making varies considerably from case-to-case and according to the particular institution involved, it is helpful to root a discussion of the integration of scientific and technical information into public decision making in a common model, or set of models. Second, and more specifically, these scenarios depict how conventional methods and procedures are employed in attempts to fold scientific or technical information into public decisions, especially when that information is disputed. Finally, by basing these hypothetical scenarios on actual cases in which consensus-based procedures were used, the contrasts between the effects of conventional and consensus-based procedures on the dynamics of decision making which are discussed further on are sharpened.

Decision Making by Elected Officials: Local Decision Making on Appropriations for a Public Project

The first hypothetical decision making scenario describes decision making by elected officials. In this case, the body of elected officials is New York

City's Board of Estimate (BOE), which is a council comprising the five elected borough presidents, the city comptroller, and the mayor. Other examples of bodies of elected decision makers include the United States Congress, state legislatures, and city councils chosen through citywide elections.

We might imagine that traditionally, local decision making by elected officials occurs much as it did in the New York City case up to the point of a "policy dialogue" (which will be described in Chapter 3) that was sponsored by the New York Academy of Sciences (NYAS). The particular decision under consideration by the BOE concerned a comprehensive municipal solid waste management plan drawn by the city's Department of Sanitation and the first leg of this plan, a facility slated for a site at the former Brooklyn Navy Yard. The BOE has the authority to approve or withhold city funds for capital projects.

First, a little background on the controversy. In 1984, New York City's 10 million residents generated an estimated 26,000 tons of municipal solid wastes (MSW) (New York City Department of Sanitation, 1984b). As the first step of a comprehensive waste management plan for the city, the Department of Sanitation (DOS) proposed to build one of eight mass-burn incinerators at the site of the former Brooklyn Navy Yard. The DOS proposal touted the mass burn technology as "one of the most successful and highly used [designs] in the world" (New York City Department of Sanitation, 1984b: 1-1) and cleverly called the facility a "resource recovery facility" because it is designed to produce electricity from the steam produced during the combustion process. The proposal, as presented to the BOE, and the accompanying letter from the DOS director prefaced the project description with dire projections of increasing daily tonnage of solid wastes, diminishing landfills, and vanishing waste disposal alternatives, painting the possibility of an impending crisis (New York City Department of Sanitation, 1984b). Then Sanitation Commissioner Steisel predicted that the one remaining landfill would be exhausted in 13 years (*New York Times*, December 7, 1984), in a city in which even publicly acceptable projects, such as schools and firehouses, commonly take six to eight years to implement, thereby implying that the city was running out of time to act.

The city's concern over the waste disposal issue was long-standing and can be traced to the first Lindsay administration, when the DOS began to anticipate the depletion of landfill sites. Proposals were drawn up, but no action was taken. Then, under the Beame administration in 1977, a "blue ribbon" task force produced a report on the city's waste management options. Although this report was not itself considered a "master plan," its overview and evaluation of alternatives for waste disposal provided the basis for the city's more recent comprehensive plan and facility site-selections. After receiving the green light from the state legislature and approval by the city's Board of Estimate (BOE), the city had in hand by 1981 a proposal for the design, construction, and operation of the first of eight proposed so-called resource recovery plants, a 3,000 tons per day capacity facility at the Brooklyn Navy Yard. The city's investment in the mass-burn incinerator thus was not trivial and was performed with sanctions and support from state as well as city government.

The Brooklyn Navy Yard site covers 13 acres in the northeastern corner of the Brooklyn Navy Yard, bordering the East River (NYC DOS. 1984b). The site is presently for the storage of road salt, sanitation trucks, and retired city vehicles and is surrounded by other industrial lands and active residential neighborhoods to the east (Williamsburg) and south (Fort Green). As proposed, the MSW incinerator would consist of four units, each capable of burning 750 tons per day and comprising an individual combustion chamber (furnace), boiler, air pollution control device (a fabric filter, or baghouse), and ash handling equipment. The four units would share one, 500-foot emission stack. Wastes would be loaded into the facility from barges, and fed onto a system of moving grates contained in the furnace. Steam generated from the combustion process would furnish energy to operate the plant and excess steam (77 percent if operated at full capacity) would be sold and exported off-site (to a nearby utility).

In addition to setting a receptive climate (in this case, depicting an impending garbage crisis) for decision makers to hear their requests, proposing agencies, especially at the local level, now routinely attempt to generate public support and anticipate and, if possible, dissipate opposition before formally presenting proposals. Public information meetings and citizen advisory committees are two common methods of attempting to achieve these aims. Through such meetings, proposing agencies present their proposals and receive comments back from "the public." The degree to which these comments result in alterations of the original proposal varies. The key point is that "the public" (at least some part of it) speaks and the agency listens. The DOS both convened periodic public information meetings as well as assembled prominent community leaders to form a citizens advisory committee in 1981.

Public comments in local decision making for public projects are also solicited through the environmental impact review process. The federal National Environmental Policy Act (NEPA) requires the preparation of an environmental impact statement (EIS) for any "major" federal action "significantly affecting the quality of the human environment" (National Environmental Policy Act, Section 4331). Many states, including New York, followed the enactment of NEPA with state legislation that more broadly requires environmental impact assessments for a wider variety of project actions. A public works proposal would virtually always require an environmental assessment and because impact statements largely consist of a collection of predictions about probable effects, and because predictions are, by nature, probabilistic and uncertain, they are wide open for dispute (Bacow) and very often become the center of public debate.[1]

The New York City case was no different. Predictably, opposition to the project emerged from many corners of the city. Paramount among the concerns raised was the fact that, unfortunately, this mass-burn technology is also known to emit a class of highly toxic chemicals known as dioxins.[2] Dioxin played in national headlines in the United States as a result of controversy over the Vietnam war sprayings of "Agent Orange," (a defoliant containing dioxins as a contaminant), and the Times Beach tragedy, (in which soil contaminated with dioxins resulted in the relocation of an entire Missouri town) and the Environmental Protection Agency (EPA) once called dioxins "one of the most perplexing and potentially dangerous chemicals ever to pollute the environment" (Raloff: 26).[3] Although their precise toxicity is unknown, dioxins have been associated with cancer, birth defects, immune system disorders, and a host of other abnormalities in laboratory animals.

The DOS-commissioned draft environmental impact statement (DEIS) was criticized sharply for failing to address adequately the human health risk posed by dioxin emissions from the proposed Brooklyn Navy Yard incinerator. Interestingly, the challenge did not come from the DOS-initiated Citizens Advisory Committee (CAC), which had been given $85,000 by the DOS to hire a technical consultant to review the document (Steisel). Up to this point, most of the CAC's concerns had centered on typical not-in-my-backyard ("NIMBY") concerns: bad odors, noise, traffic congestion, and so on. Instead, the objections to the DEIS stemmed largely from reports prepared by the Center for the Biology of Natural Systems (CBNS), Queens College, whose assistance had been requested by the Williamsburg community adjacent to the Brooklyn Navy Yard site.

The BOE's reaction to the strong criticism differed little from the conventional response of elected decision makers. They simply requested further examination of the issue. In this case, the proposal was sent back to the DOS, which responded predictably by contracting with an outside consultant to undertake a new study to address the health risks specifically.

The heat of the controversy encouraged BOE members to delay their decision for several months. Meanwhile, other minor policy actors entered the fray. The *New York Times* printed editorials urging BOE members to approve the project (*New York Times*, October 15, 1984; December 20, 1984; July 8, 1985; August 15, 1985). Environmental groups expressed reservations about the project at public forums and in letters and comments in local papers (*New York Times*, November 17, 1984; August 4, 1985; August 15, 1985) and advocated greater investment by the city in alternatives such as recycling and source reduction approaches to waste management.

The headline story on the proposal, however, from the issuance of the CBNS report onward, focused on the health risks of dioxin emissions.

One can also assume during this interval that BOE members were approached by their constituency including special interest groups and the voters in their district. The Brooklyn Navy Yard waste processing plant was one of eight similar facilities identified in the DOS's comprehensive solid waste management plan for sites strategically dispersed throughout the city in order to deflect community concerns about social equity. As such, it represented the first leg of a huge capital expenditure project estimated to cost $3 billion (*New York Times*, December 7, 1984), and the construction industry, among others, no doubt would be hungry for the lucrative project. Mayor Koch had also voiced solid support for the project, after having recently lost a long battle for the highly capital-intensive "Westway" project. It is fair to expect, as one participant claimed, that the Mayor's office was vigorously lobbying individual BOE members, especially political allies who courted the Mayor's endorsement in their reelection campaigns.[4]

In September 1984, the DOS-commissioned report, performed by Fred C. Hart & Associates (hereinafter referred to as "the Hart report") was issued. Although projecting a higher risk than the original DEIS, the risk estimates of the Hart report were still much closer to those in the initial DEIS than to the CBNS predictions. Objections to the facility were not put to rest, however. Thus, after a series of conventional public hearings, the formation of a citizen's advisory committee, and an effort to quell public controversy through an "authoritative" expert report, the elected decision makers continued to face an angry, confused, and suspicious public.

Administrative Decision Making: Traditional Rulemaking

Many state and federal agencies routinely engage in science-intensive decision making on issues inherently linked to science, such as health, safety, and environmental regulation. Although the details of decision making may vary according to an agency's internal operating procedures and specific legislative statutes, there are similarities in the ways they handle scientific or technical disagreement. To broadly illustrate this decision making pathway, consider how the Environmental Protection Agency (EPA) would have gone about setting new source performance standards for wood stoves emissions.

On August 2, 1985, the Environmental Protection Agency issued an "advanced notice of proposed rulemaking" for performance standards for new stationary sources of particulate emissions from residential wood combustion (RWC) units. EPA estimated that as of the end of 1983, 10.6 million RWC units, defined as freestanding woodstoves and fireplace inserts, were putting out 2.7 million tons of particulate matter (PM), including 20,000 tons of polycyclic organic matter (POM), 7.4 million tons of carbon monoxide (CO), and 62,000 tons of hydrocarbon (HC) emissions annually (*Federal Register*, 1985). The annual sales of new RWC units was projected to continue at 1 million units per year.

In addition to the deterioration of air quality noted in several locales where a high number of wood burning devices and geographic conditions were believed to seriously aggravate air pollution, the EPA recognized the adverse health impact caused by particulate emissions. According to studies of ambient total suspended particulate (TSP) levels, RWC units were estimated to account for from 66 to 84 percent of the smaller respirable particulates.

The catalyst for EPA action was a legal suit filed by the State of New York and the Natural Resources Defense Council following the Agency's decision not to list POM as a hazardous air pollutant under Section 112 of the Clean Air Act. Since RWC units are believed to account for nearly half of total nationwide POM, the litigants agreed to settle the suit if, among other provisions, EPA promulgated new source performance standards (NSPS) for particulate matter for RWC units.

EPA's traditional procedure for promulgating new source performance standards under the Clean Air Act relies heavily on staff in the technical branch of the Standards and Development Branch.[5] An imaginary scenario for developing emission standards for wood stoves under the traditional procedure would begin with Branch staff initiating a search for relevant technical information, beginning with a survey of the published literature, and reaching out to segments of the industry for opportunities to familiarize themselves with wood stoves production, sales, and use. On-site visits of production facilities nearby is also an option. The identification of firms solicited for input would be biased somewhat in accordance with physical proximity and the personal familiarity of Branch staff with individual firm names or personnel.

EPA is required by law to publish its intention to promulgate new rules. This formal public announcement often signals the starting point for informal lobbying by stakeholding groups. Typically, as the soon-to-be regulated industry gets wind of EPA intentions, either individual companies or trade groups attempt to influence the shaping of the EPA document by (selectively) contributing technical and manufacturing information and volunteering other opinions and ideas. Major environmental groups that specialize in clean air issues, such as the Natural Resources Defence Council (NRDC), would also try to keep their finger on the pulse of EPA efforts. Compared with industry efforts, however, environmental group lobbying efforts tend to center on influencing the interpretation of the regulatory intent of relevant legislation, rather than contributing additional technical information, reflecting the organizations' own area of expertise and lack of technical resources.

During the pre-proposal stage, lobbying activity, which is sometimes quite heavy,[6] is dominated disproportionately by certain groups. Interest groups with Washington D.C. offices and staff who personally interact with EPA on a regular basis appear to have greater access to EPA decision making than more distant, potentially affected interests. Also, public interest groups with organizational support and experience with air pollution issues are more likely to become involved at early stages than public interest groups with lesser resources or other specialties (like consumer's rights). In the wood stoves case, the NRDC staff knew early on about the agency's rulemaking intentions from the out-of-court settlement and, presumably, could begin informal lobbying with EPA staff ahead of other interest groups. In fact, representatives from the NRDC and the industry's Wood Heating Alliance (WHA), both with offices located within blocks of one another and not far from EPA headquarter offices in Washington, D.C., discussed the rulemaking procedures with one another and independently with EPA before the public announcement of the agency's intention to promulgate rules was issued. Situational factors plus physical proximity thus enabled these two groups to have a jump on other interested parties regarding communications with the agency.

On the other hand, groups holding relevant technical information and expertise may not be sufficiently motivated to lobby at the pre-proposal stage. In the wood stoves case, for example, the independent testing laboratories had unique experience and expertise in testing emissions from wood stoves as a result of business generated by the Oregon and Colorado state regulations. For the individual testing firms, however, the wood stoves tests probably produced only a fraction of their total revenues providing them little incentive, financial or otherwise, to allocate staff time and resources toward developing EPA regulations. Thus, a potential gold mine of experience, expertise, and data would be left untouched. Similarly, the states of Oregon and Colorado had a wealth of regulatory and technical knowledge gained through their state-level regulatory experiences. Representatives from both states, however, expressed doubt that (their own) agency budgets would have allowed their involvement in conventional rulemaking proceedings beyond simply reacting and sending in written comments to EPA's proposed rules.[7]

Before the proposed rules are published in the *Federal Register*, staff in various branches of the agency review the proposal for aspects of the rules which pertain especially to their branch. For example, staff in the Enforcement and Compliance Division would review the proposed rules for language clarity, consistency, and general enforceability. Agency legal advisors would read through the proposed rules for consistency and conformance with enabling statutes. Each set of comments would be incorporated into a subsequent draft rule and sent around again for review to the various branches. This rather lengthy and circuitous review route typically undergoes at least three cycles. Syntheses of the various comments is largely the responsibility of the Standards and Development Branch.

Once the agency stamp of approval is given, the rules are published in the *Federal Register* and made available for public review and comment. The public is given 60 days to read the proposed rules, submit written comments, and request a public hearing. At the end of the 60-day period, written comments are distributed to relevant branches in the agency for yet another round of review and comment. A public hearing, if requested by a member of the public, allows individuals to express their concerns and argue their positions in person before EPA staff. Again, it is the responsibility and choice of the Standards and Development Branch to evaluate the significance of all public and in-house comments and to integrate them into the final rules. The promulgation of major rules in this manner typically takes from three to five years. Administrative rulemaking is open to judicial challenge (after formal promulgation), however, and in 1984, four out of five regulations proposed by EPA were contested in court (Susskind and McMahon), with about 30 percent of litigated rules significantly changed as a result.

Judicial Decision Making

Litigation in the fields of environmental protection, resource management, occupational health and safety, and consumer product safety often turns on particular scientific or technical assessments of impacts, likelihood of impacts, and magnitudes of harm. In judicial decision making, the decision maker may be either a jury of citizens, one judge, or a panel of judges. For example, personal injury lawsuits are judged by juries, while "mass toxic torts" cases, such as the suits against the Johns-Mansville Corporation by asbestos workers, and lawsuits against the actions of administrative agencies are handled largely by courts without juries. Since a large proportion of the science-intensive lawsuits involve regulatory disputes, our discussion of judicial decision making will concentrate on administrative law.

In the United States, the courts may review challenged federal administrative, rulemaking decisions for three points: (1) to ensure that the agency acted within its mandated authority; (2) to ensure the agency's actions were procedurally consistent with relevant laws; and (3) to ascertain whether the agency's action was arbitrary and capricious. One legal scholar describes the role of the judiciary as follows:

> [T]he court has a supervisory function of review of agency decisions. This begins with enforcing the requirement of reasonable procedure, fair notice,

and opportunity for the parties to present their case, and it includes examining the evidence and fact findings to see both that the evidentiary fact findings are supported by the record and that they provide a rational basis for inferences of ultimate fact (Levanthal: 511).

The precise basis for a court's review is dependent on the claims filed in the lawsuit. A judicial review on the basis of the first two points is clearly within the court's area of expertise; the third point is more problematic, since understanding whether a decision is "arbitrary and capricious" may require a close review of highly sophisticated technical argumentation whereas judges in the U.S. are largely trained as generalists who work their way up the ranks of the legal system. Their lack of specialized knowledge and training necessary for understanding complex technical arguments is aggravated by the time pressure on court decisions imposed by the long list of cases waiting to be heard, as well as the scarcity of resources allocated to the court for technical consultancy.

As a result of the court's awareness of its limited technical capabilities, a court ruling on the "arbitrary and capricious" standard commonly restricts its examination only to determine whether the agency decision was based on "sufficient" scientific data and reasoning.[8] In one suit by chemical and gasoline manufacturers challenging EPA's regulations requiring the phased reduction of lead in gasoline, the opinion of the U.S. Court of Appeals, District of Columbia, expressed outright that the proper function of the court is to examine the technical evidence "*solely* to enable the court to determine whether the agency decision was rational and based on consideration of relevant factors" (*Ethyl Corporation v. EPA*); [italics in original]. In other words, that two or more equally "rational" technical arguments may justify contradictory policy prescriptions is inconsequential to the judicial reviewer. The court explained that

> evidence may be isolated that supports virtually any inference one might care to draw. Thus we might well have sustained a determination by the Administrator *not* to regulate lead additives on health grounds. That does not mean, however, that we cannot sustain his determination to so regulate (*Ethyl Corporation v. EPA*) [italics in original].

Hence, as long as the court can find no fault with the agency's line of reasoning, the court will affirm the agency's decision.

Similarly, in a suit against the EPA in which the plaintiff contested the scientific basis for EPA regulatory standards, the U.S. First Circuit Court concluded that petitioner's contention that contrary conclusions can be drawn from the data does not lead us to suspect that EPA committed clear error. To the extent [that] different conclusions could be drawn, the Agency was entitled to draw its own (*South Terminal Corporation v. EPA*).

The reluctance of the court to extend beyond its scope of expertise is understandable given its shortfalls in expertise and time, but it does not promise that the courts will deliver scientifically sound resolutions to technically complex litigation.

Our example of a litigation case involving scientific arguments is a highly emotional conflict over fishing in Michigan's Great Lakes. This fishing dispute had a long history, formalized in 1973 when the first legal suit was filed. The United States government on behalf of the Bay Mills Indian Community[9] (and later joined as intervenors by the tribe itself, and the Sault St. Marie Tribe and the Grand Traverse Band of Ottawa-Chippewa Indians[10]) sued the State of Michigan over its jurisdictional authority to regulate tribal fishers in the Great Lakes of Michigan, Huron and Superior.

In response to grave concern over the lake ecology and the extermination of the indigenous lake trout first noted in the 1940s, the United States Fish and Wildlife Service (FWS) and the state of Michigan Department of Natural Resources (DNR) embarked on aggressive fishery management programs beginning in the 1960s. The primary objective of both agencies was the rehabilitation of the lake trout, and a cooperative arrangement was worked out in which the FWS provided DNR with fish for annual planting. Although lake trout were found to thrive in many parts of the lake, it was widely believed that reproduction was not occurring.

DNR's management approach grew increasingly aggressive. According to one legal counsel, DNR management practice was "regulating commercial fishing out of business." Among the most controversial and provocative restrictions imposed by the DNR was the banning of large mesh gill nets, which was intended to reduce the incidental catch of lake trout in areas fished commercially for white fish. Gill net gear was used by all small boat commercial fishers, but it was an integral part of tribal fishing culture. Moreover, the alternative trap net gear requiring large boats is beyond the reach of poorly capitalized tribal fishers. From the tribes' perspective the ban constituted a direct threat on their lifestyle and livelihood. (In fact, many non-tribal small boat commercial fishers were put out of business by the gill net ban.) It was the enforcement of this ban against tribal fishers that triggered the 1973 lawsuit, leading to a ruling, in 1979, that decreed that an 1836 treaty protected the non-exclusive fishing rights of the tribes and that the tribes held the right to fish free of regulations imposed by the State of Michigan, unless the State could prove that tribal fishing was endangering the resource (*United States v. Michigan*, 1980).

Subsequent to the 1979 court ruling, the three tribal communities cooperatively set up their own fishery regulatory program called the Chippewa-Ottawa Fishery Management Authority with a grant from the U.S. Bureau of Indian Affairs. Subsumed under the Authority was a staff of biologists charged with monitoring tribal fishing activities and its impact on the fishery and advising the tribal leaders on management issues. The tribal management program served a dual purpose. First, it started the tribes on a path toward regulating tribal fishing activities consistent with the fishery resource and, second, it brought the tribes closer to dealing with the federal and state governments on more equal footing by enabling them to speak more fluently in the "language" of fish biologists and resource managers.

Also about the same time, biologists concerned about the status of the Great Lakes fishery representing the DNR, the FWS, and the tribes began to meet informally annually to develop "total allowable catch" (TAC) figures for various lake species. TAC is based on estimates of a number of factors such as fish population size, age structure, growth rate, and mortality rate. Many of these estimates were based on data contributed by the members of this "tripartite technical working group" (TTWG), including, for example, catch data for past years provided by FWS to whom both the state and tribal fishers reported. The annual status report published by this group represented a compilation of data from the various parties and a rough consensus on the levels of catch any particular population could sustain.

During the early years of the 1980s fishing on the Great Lakes intensified. In response to an aggressive state tourism promotion effort, sport fishing flourished. The tribal fishing industry rebounded from past lows in part as a result of the favorable court ruling on treaty rights. Predictably, as fishing by all parties increased, fishery managers noted the approach and passing of TACs at earlier and earlier points in the season between 1980 and 1984.

The surpassing of TACs fixed by the Tripartite Technical Working Group set off tensions between the DNR and the tribes and tribal and non-tribal fishers anew. On a few occasions the tribes closed their fisheries, inducing tribal fishers to migrate to more distant or less familiar waters. The predominantly small boat tribal fishers shared an affinity with recreational fishers for sheltered bays and shore areas of the vast lakes. Although tribal fishers, like non-tribal commercial fishers, primarily sought whitefish, their large mesh gill nets were suspected of indiscriminately killing the sport fishers' preferred lake trout. Gill nets also can snag the sport fishers' angler gear, a fact which undoubtedly contributed to the frustration that led to incidences of vandalism against gill nets set out in the waters. Tempers rose on the water and non-fishing tribal members on land suffered a backlash of hostile reactions.

On other occasions the tribes asked the court to order the closing of fishing waters to state-licensed, commercial fishers, agreeing to prohibit tribal fishing in those same waters concurrently with the court order. Such actions reportedly incited tribal and non-tribal fishers alike to fish as intensively as possible before the fishery was closed, creating what has been called a "racehorse fishery."

Why did the DNR not close the state fishery when TACs were reached? While acknowledging on one hand the value of setting TACs, the DNR did not believe that managing by TACs was effective, efficient, or desirable. DNR preferred to manage according to "total allowable effort" (TAE), meaning to regulate the number of fishing licenses, not the number of fish caught. The state argued that fishers routinely underreport their catch to officials, resulting in inaccurate catch reports. Since fishery personnel have a fairly clear idea of how many fish can be caught over a given period of time using a given type of gear, DNR resource managers argued that a more accurate approach is to divide TACs by the average catch by gear type and limit the number of licenses per zone, accordingly.

Theoretically, TAE and TAC are equivalent measures, but from a management perspective, they differ substantially. Under the TAE management approach, licenses are assigned to specific zones and the closing of certain lake zones could put affected state-licensed fishers out of work for the season. Consequently, even if TACs are overshot before the end of the season, the state was reluctant to close the fishery. By choosing to manage by TAE, the state risked facing the possibility of trading-off an incremental depletion of the fishery resource for the economic stability of state-licensed fishers.

A second, more legalistic reason for the DNR's inaction was the state's interpretation of its administrative code, which would require a public hearing and a 90-day waiting period before a fishery could be closed. Under this interpretation, a federal court order was the only route sufficiently expedient to avert overfishing.

By 1984, it became apparent to the tribal fishers that additional court intervention was necessary in the management of the fishing resource and to reduce hostilities and violence.[11] The tribes filed a motion for the court to allocate the fish catch. Although the optimum division from the perspective of the tribes was humorously described as allowing "non-Indians to get the heads and the tails," when they filed for the motion, they were actually hoping for a 50-50 split across the board (all lake areas and all fish species). In contrast, the DNR was concerned that a 50-50 split of all fish ignored their own efforts at restoring fish populations, particularly in respect to the lake trout "put-grow-take" fishery. DNR staff also suspected serious underreporting of incidental lake trout catches by tribal gill net fishers, which would result in higher actual catches for the tribal fishers.

The presiding judge, Judge Enslen, ordered the parties to negotiate a settlement, which they ultimately did successfully. If the parties had not been asked to negotiate an agreement, however, and the judge was required to rule on the issue, what would have been the basis of his ruling?

It is likely that Judge Enslen would have looked first to history for legal precedents set by similar resource allocation disputes. As reported in an article in *Legal Times*, "previous judicial resolutions of such disputes have generally divided the resource 'down the middle,' making no one happy and usually prolonging the battle."[12] If Judge Enslen had decided to resolve the case by ordering a percentage division of the resource, the critical issue would be how the judge defined the resource. Would he define it as the lakes' fishing areas or as total fish stock? Discussions among the parties prior to the 1984 litigation had mentioned both a "zone concept" for assigning exclusive fishing areas according to "historically established, discrete fish populations," and a straight 50-50 split of fish according to species and zones. Would the judge's definition of the resource include only naturally reproducing fish populations, or would planted fish also be counted?

Whatever the principle Judge Enslen selected for deriving his allocation scheme, if he ultimately defined the resource as fish stocks, eventually he would need a set of data to describe the fishery (population sizes, age structures, migration patterns, mortality, etc.). Here again his decision process would grow murky, since his reliance on one set of data over another would have no objective basis. Each litigating party would have submitted their version of a "comprehensive inventory" of the fishery. How would he choose among the data? In many cases data would be incomplete. In some cases, data would be conflicting. And, more than likely, each side would vehemently contest the validity of data provided by the other.

For example, one sensitive issue was the extent to which large mesh gill net fishing depleted the lake trout populations. Assumptions about gill net-induced mortality affect the estimation of catch levels. The defendant, the Michigan Department of Natural Resources (DNR), claimed that the catch reports submitted by the tribal fishers seriously understated actual catches. Undoubtedly, the state's attorney would submit testimony by DNR fisheries division biologists attesting to the high probability that these reports were inaccurate, making various technical arguments why higher catch levels should be expected (including, perhaps, results from location specific assessment studies). Lacking the resources to go out and repeat similar assessment studies (which require actual catching and counting of fish), or the time and resources to monitor the actual fish catch of tribal fishers, the judge would have no scientific basis for accepting one catch level figure over the other. Yet, in order for him to issue a finding and order, he would be forced to assume the accuracy of one set of data over the other, or to simply "split the difference" between the two catch level estimates. None of his options would be clearly superior from a scientific perspective.[13]

Methods for Handling Scientific Information

These brief decision making scenarios illustrate several approaches commonly applied in conventional decision making to facilitate the exchange of information. Procedures for gathering information from the public and, more pointedly, for resolving disagreement on scientific components of public issues are highly similar across the three, different institutional settings. These methods by *technique*, however, create barriers to a full airing and reconciliation of disputed scientific and technical points and contested political claims and, in fact, encourage a distortion of the issues and debate.

Limited Repertoire of Methods

The methods for handling scientific and technical information applied in various forums of public decision making can be divided roughly into two categories: those designed to elicit information and those designed to settle explicit disagreement. Public information meetings, public hearings (and court hearings), and written comments (and legal briefs, including those submitted by *amici curiae*), are examples of procedures for eliciting comments on relevant scientific and technical components of public issues, as well as on more general aspects. Newspaper editorials and letters-to-the-editor are additional mechanisms by which interested parties can express their positions and concerns to the decision maker. These methods share a common model of dynamics and relationships. In this model, the decision maker receives comments from stakeholders. The comments consist of arguments in favor of or in opposition to a particular policy position or decision alternative. Often, these "position" comments will be accompanied by scientific or technical arguments that show that the advocated position is consistent with scientific knowledge (although sometimes the advocated position may be no more than a refutation of a proposed decision alternative without supportive technical data or arguments.) This model is presented schematically in Figure 2.1.

In the New York City case, the Board of Estimate is the decision maker who receives arguments supporting and opposing the Brooklyn Navy Yard plant. In this case, the DOS is considered a stakeholder, as are the CAC, the CBNS, and individuals and groups expressing their viewpoints through the media. In the wood stoves case, the EPA as a whole is the decision maker; WHA, the NRDC, and other groups who submit written comments or speak at public hearings are stakeholders. Finally, in litigation like the

The Dynamics of Advocacy Science 29

Figure 2.1
Communication Flows in Conventional
Information–Eliciting Procedures

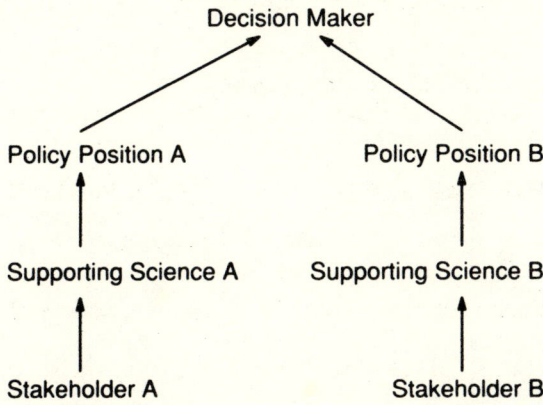

Michigan case, the judge is the decision maker, and the litigants and *amici curiae* are the stakeholders.[14]

Often the scientific or technical support for an undesired decision or decision alternative is targeted for attack by competing stakeholders. In these cases, the scientific disagreement becomes the major focus of the challenge. In the New York City case, for example, the risk posed by dioxin emissions became the primary issue. Questions pertaining to the level of expected dioxin emissions, (a "scientific" question), became salient. In the Michigan case, reported fish catches, which provided raw data for estimating population mortality were contested.

When parties introduce scientific and technical analysis that is at odds with those that support competing decision alternatives, decision makers sometimes respond by employing a second tier of methods intended to reconcile contradictory technical claims. This group of methods relies on consultation with experts, either individuals or panels, either verbally or through more formal, written reports, or some mixture of the two. This approach is presented schematically in Figure 2.2. In this case, the "expert" examines the scientific and technical evidence presented by the stakeholders, as well as additional information identified independently, and reports to the decision maker. Presumably, the report focusses primarily on disputed scientific and technical components of the policy issue. In the New York City case, the Hart report represented an attempt to consult an "expert" who would be authoritative. In a conventional EPA rulemaking process, a committee on the Science Advisory Board might serve as an internal "expert" review panel.

Figure 2.2
Communication Flows in Conventional
Dispute Resolution Procedures

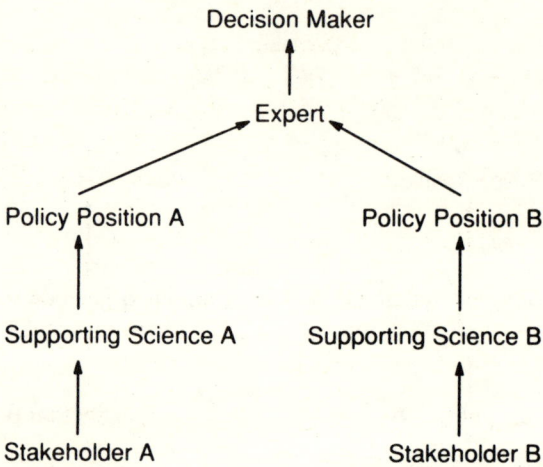

The implementability and political popularity of this approach is indicated by the routinized character of expert review committees. Organizations such as the National Academy of Science (NAS) assemble special task forces to review existing scientific information on important issues of policy significance and report on their findings on demand. The NAS has convened task forces to arbitrate technical disagreements on issues relating to policy to reduce airborne lead, to protect the ozone layer, and on the biological effects of low-level ionizing radiation, to name just a few. Administrative agencies, such as EPA and the Occupational Safety and Health Administration (OSHA), are permitted by law to create "permanent," "quasi-permanent," and "*ad hoc*" advisory committees to provide expert advice on general and specific policy issues.

In the courtroom, a parallel method is represented by the practice of appointing a "special master." Judges faced with technically complex litigation sometimes enlist the aid of a "special master" who has training in a pertinent technical field. In most cases, the special master is asked simply to review technical documents submitted by the litigants and *amici curiae,* although he is free to supplement the information with additional research of his own, thus broadening the scope of information that ultimately provides the basis for his opinion on important technical issues. The use of special masters also enhances the court's ability to deal with science-intensive disputes by bringing down conventional barriers such as limitations on *ex parte* communication (Little). In any case, the special master ultimately serves as yet another interpreter of disputed scientific and technical facts, advising the judge accordingly. His "break-the-tie" opinion, like the expert panel or neutral report, often then becomes the authority on which the court bases its broader, legal decision.

Finally, public agencies anticipating citizen opposition to an action or project commonly employ a third method which is procedurally more flexible than other methods and which, therefore, does not fall neatly into either of the two general approaches outlined above. This method is the formation of a citizen advisory committee. The citizen advisory committee differs from expert task forces or review panels because persons without particularly relevant technical expertise may participate. Rather than relevant technical expertise constituting the overriding criterion for appointment, political credentials guide the selection of the membership of citizen advisory committees, with "the opposition" represented commonly by the least radical elements.[15] The DOS exercised this strategy as the sponsor of the controversial waste disposal plan. The DOS's citizen advisory committee accordingly comprised two borough presidents and other respected community spokespersons.

In instances in which disagreement on scientific or technical components is expected or, in fact, does intensify debate over a policy issue, the citizen advisory committee is awarded funds to conduct a review of the information. Under the Massachusetts Hazardous Waste Facility Siting Act, potential host communities of hazardous waste facilities are eligible to apply for technical assistance grants to enable them to hire necessary expertise to review baseline study materials as well as the preliminary environmental impact statement. In the New York City case, the citizen's advisory committee hired a consultant (with DOS funds) to review the DOS proposal, including the DEIS.

The gamble taken by the decision maker or, in the New York City case, the sponsoring agency, is that the committee may end up opposing the preferred decision alternative. The Brooklyn Navy Yard citizen's advisory committee eventually concurred with the findings in the project proposal, but in other cases, the citizen's advisory committee's consultants may uncover points worthy of serious debate, and may end up causing the project proposer or the agency additional delays and costs. A more skeptical view of the intent behind establishing citizen advisory committees suggests that such cases would be rare, however, because citizen advisory committees can become "coopted" (Selznick). Cooptation can occur when the project sponsor is allowed to "wine and dine" the members of the citizen advisory committee or through close fraternizing with agency staff, as committee members begin to share the values and objectives of the project sponsor or the agency.

Common Roots: Implications of Logical Positivist Empiricism

These methods for managing scientific and technical information in public decision making, especially ones that attempt to "resolve" challenges to scientific premises, share a common theoretical lineage. The underlying assumption of these procedures is the logical positivist empiricist view of science in which scientific knowledge is defined as politically neutral and objective. The logical positivist empiricist view suggests that any disagreement between scientists is due to error. For example, discrepancies between data are presumed attributable to error in experimental procedure. On a grander scale, the development of two contradictory or competing theories is presumed due to one theoretician's incomplete review of available data. And, disagreement on the meaning of research findings is attributed to faulty logic. Short of these sources of error, disagreement is explained by error due to the personal bias of one (or more) scientist who has allowed personal objectives to inappropriately enter and distort his analysis.

In this framework, disputed scientific points that arise in the context of public decision making ought to be resolved by uncovering error. Since error ought to be detected and corrected by a careful review of competing scientific arguments (to verify data and retrace the logic leading to the two [or more] incompatible conclusions) a reasonable approach to handling disagreement on scientific aspects of a decision is to conduct an additional review of the contradictory scientific arguments. In theory, the review should reveal error and determine which analysis can be proven scientifically invalid, and which can not. Expert review panels and hiring additional consultants are procedures that are consistent with this approach to conflicting technical documentation. The science court is another example, one that has been reintroduced periodically by supporters over the past 20 years. As initially proposed, a "science court" would consist of a judge or panel of judges who would adjudicate scientific "right and wrong" after advocates of competing scientific views present their strongest arguments (Kantrowitz). The fundamental presumption of these types of procedures is that scientific knowledge is unified and properly undertaken scientific experimentation produces data and findings that are unambiguous and consistent with the results of coexisting studies.

Structuring the Use of Science and Its Consequences

As the New York City case shows, conventional methods for integrating public comment, including scientific and technical information, into politically acceptable and scientifically sound decisions can miss the mark. Despite the project sponsor's use of public hearings, public meetings, the EIS process to solicit written comments, and a citizen advisory committee, challenges to the project's scientific and technical premises were not dispelled. The decision making Board of Estimate's final attempt to quiet health risk concerns was to order the Department of Sanitation to commission a new study by independent consultants whose report they hoped the public would view as neutral. They were wrong, and the controversy continued.

These methods fail on two counts. First, they provide neither a context nor a structure conducive to a comprehensive review of scientific and technical information nor for settling disagreements on scientific or technical points that arise. Instead, these procedures encourage policy stakeholders to present technical information in a purely self-interested, highly selective manner. Secondly, and more fundamentally, these methods do not encourage decision makers to address the full range of political disagreements that stands behind contentious political debates. All attention remains focussed on the disagreements over technical issues, which is itself a political act to avoid public participation at a more meaningful level. At best, these methods simply fail to provide opportunities for clarifying either scientific or political views. At worst, these methods cultivate an adversarial use of science that serves to obfuscate the political nature of public conflict.

The failure of these methods for handling scientific information is explained by three major factors. First, the technical basis of scientific disagreement remains hidden, from both the decision maker and, possibly, the competing stakeholders. Second, by failing to integrate the consideration of scientific and political aspects of a policy issue, the political interests that drive participation by stakeholding groups are left unaddressed. Finally, the role cast for the scientist raises concerns about credibility that cannot be adequately put to rest. Each of these points are elaborated on more fully below.

Basis of Scientific Disagreement Remains Hidden

Procedures that are commonly used in conventional decision making institutions, namely public comment, public hearings, court hearings and the submission of legal briefs, provide opportunities for stakeholding groups to bring to the attention of decision makers scientific or technical evidence that might induce the decision maker (and others) to support or oppose a particular decision alternative. The anatomy of these methods, however, shows that incentives or mechanisms for parties to uncover the basis of contending scientific or technical evidence are lacking. The primary function of these methods is to persuade decision makers, not to educate or establish a common understanding of important elements of the decision (McCarthy). This narrow objective has a number of consequences.

Parties are rewarded for the self-interested orchestration of information. They present technical information to support their preferred decision alternative, or to undermine a competing one in an explicit attempt to appeal to the authoritative power of science. When cross-examination of technical witnesses is allowed in the courtroom or at public hearings, questioning is directed again toward bolstering one's own analyses or discrediting opposing analyses, rather than attempting to establish any kind of enlightened consensus. As Nyhart and Carrow have written, adversarial proceedings are characterized by, "one party with witnesses striving to prove facts essential to her or his case and the other party striving to disprove those facts" (Nyhart and Carrow: 3). In this context, neither party has a clear incentive to introduce evidence that does not support its claims. In fact, such information may be treated as extraneous, even by the decision maker. As a result, scientific studies whose findings may bridge the gap between disparate technical arguments and forge a sound basis for decision making remain excluded from the record (Abrams and Berry).

Second, these methods share serious constraints on communication that obstruct the revelation of the technical basis of disagreement on scientific or technical components. Written comments submitted to decision makers are strictly one-way channels of communication. Hearings allow only limited communications between the decision maker and stakeholders, and among stakeholders. Although a series of public hearings may be held on any given issue, normally the sequential arrangement is intended either to address geographically distinct constituencies or to consider different aspects of the controversy. Rarely are consecutive hearings held to accommodate give-and-take discussion, with intervals between meetings to allow, if necessary, for additional research or data collection aimed at narrowing or resolving scientific disagreements. In administrative decision making, legislation intended to prevent agency "capture" prescribes strict limitations on communications between the rulemaking agency and affected parties (Susskind and Cruikshank: 35).

From the perspective of stakeholders, such limited and one-way communication breeds discontent and disillusionment. Participants in the wood stoves case consistently expressed dismay with traditional rulemaking procedures. Some likened the practice of submitting to EPA written comments on proposed rules to throwing their comments into a "black hole" or "black box." There is a general frustration and a feeling of insignificance in public comment and public hearing formats: one may yell and scream and make a highly rational and well-documented case, but one may never know who, if anyone, is listening. Under such circumstances, parties may be discouraged from initiating communications entirely.

While the formal procedure suggests that two-way communication does not occur at all, in fairness to EPA staff, discussions with non-agency persons involved frequently with federal agency rulemaking confirm that commentators are sometimes engaged informally in more in-depth, two-way communication after the public hearing or submission of written comment by agency staff committed to understanding the meaning and implications of comments.[16] The option of appointing special masters endows the court with more flexibility with regard to communications with parties over submissions of a scientific or technical nature. Whether or not two-way communication occurs, however, in both instances, is idiosyncratic and depends largely on the personalities, work load, and other factors concerning the individuals and the agency or the court.

Moreover, privately initiated communication that occurs subsequent to the "one-shot" largely "one-way" public hearing is not witnessed by other stakeholders. Thus, in addition to concerns about collusion and "back room deal making," communication conducted outside of public forums forgoes the likelihood that supplementary data, interpretations, or objections held by other parties would be discovered. And, opportunities for the cross-pollenization of information that might yield new insights is lost.

Finally, although public and judicial hearings provide stakeholders a chance to argue their position before the decision maker(s), albeit under strained and constrained conditions, the purpose of communication in such a context is explicitly to persuade, not to inform. Scientists and others citing scientific work adeptly manipulate language, accordingly. The repertoire of tactics employed by stakeholders and their expert collaborators begins with the drama constructed around the presentation of scientific information and moves on to the selection of words spoken or written in testimony (Brooks; Gusfield; Mazur).

For example, the DOS's preference for the term "resource recovery facility" to describe the proposed waste processing option purposefully evokes a benign, even environmentally positive image, whereas "mass-burn incinerator," in contrast, does not. Stakeholders presenting expert witnesses recruit not simply persons with relevant technical training, but individuals with degrees (such as Ph.D's) and titles. The list of witnesses comprising the New York City DOS's testimony before the BOE, for example, included the first administrator of the New York City Environmental Protection Administration, a former chief engineer of the Sanitation Department, and others. These degrees and titles are intended as evidence of the witness's expertise and credibility. The implication is that disagreement among scientist-witnesses should be judged on the basis of personal reputations, rather than the technical merits of contending arguments. Such a standard for evaluating competing technical arguments does little to advance the collective understanding of technical factors, or to ensure decisions are methodologically sound and consistent with the state of scientific knowledge.

Other examples of manipulative communication tactics that are tolerated, if not encouraged, in existing decision making include the use of rhetorical devices, deceptive labelling, and the strategic "packaging" of technical information. One writer has suggested that rhetorical devices are a major source of public confusion on the technical merits of decision alternatives (Mazur). Hence, when Tobacco Institute, Inc. spokespersons allege that "no scientific evidence exists to prove that cigarette smoking causes lung cancer in humans," technically-speaking, they are correct, since human epidemiological studies are impossible to conduct due to the difficulties of controlling for intervening variables. This statement does not address what is indicated from findings of other types of studies, however, such as laboratory animal experiments or statistical studies which form much of the basis for the anti-smoking campaign. Statements like that of the Tobacco Institute, Inc. spokespersons are intended to confuse decision makers and other non-expertly trained persons by appearing to refute contending scientific arguments without actually addressing their substance.

The "packaging" of technical information also sometimes has emotive significance. For example, an increase above the "normal" background risk of developing cancer to an individual over a 70-year lifetime may appear small, and could be expected to stir little response among the public. In contrast, the same increase applied to an entire population would yield an aggregate number of cancers that could appear quite worrisome. Stakeholders and experts avail of different formulas to express essentially the same information according to the response they desire.

The consequence of these communication constraints is a potentially critical flaw, namely that even a well-intentioned recipient of stakeholder comments has no mechanism for reconciling two contradictory sets of technical analyses outside of her own ability to dissect the arguments. Agency staff assigned the task of explaining discrepancies may spend days laboriously walking through the methodology and analysis of various submissions. Stakeholders may consciously obfuscate or misrepresent scientific documentation. Since the format of the scientific and technical presentation is fixed and largely the choosing of the contributor, the analyst may spend hours simply converting measurements presented in different units in competing analyses into comparable form. The quality and character of the scientific evidence presented by the disputants may be inconsistent or stakeholders may focus on entirely different points in their technical argumentation. The arduous translation may be impossible to complete, but in many cases time constraints prevent more than a cursory attempt. Yet, it is the responsibility of the reviewer to judge the relative merits of all submissions.

The Distortion of Political Concerns

Other serious concerns are also raised by procedures that focus narrowly on scientific disagreement. As noted earlier, public issues become disputes when two or more parties are dissatisfied with their assessments of change expected to result from certain policy decisions. In other words, groups mobilize for or against public decisions in accordance with their political interests, the demands they view as rightfully theirs. The policy option that a group advocates represents a position considered to meet these political interests.

Politically astute and resourceful groups are careful to develop options that are consistent with some body of scientific or technical information. While contending groups wrap their preferred policy option with supportive scientific or technical documentation, the appeal to a "tie-breaking expert" presumes that contrary scientific and technical arguments can be extracted from these packages and examined in isolation. If the "expert" finds one or more arguments to be invalid, much of the persuasive power of the corresponding policy alternative is lost. In fact, it is unlikely that the decision maker will select that option.

Although a group may err in selecting a policy alternative that is based on inaccurate analysis, incomplete data, or some other flaw in the supportive scientific arguments, their political interests are nonetheless real. A decision making method that fails to acknowledge the political interests that lie beneath the policy alternatives advocated by different groups is shortchanging the political process. In a sense, disregarding a policy alternative because the scientific or technical argument is weak is like throwing the baby out with the bath water.

Even if decision makers succeed in uncovering the basis for discrepant scientific or technical arguments, methods that attempt to deal with scientific disagreement and political interests separately do not provide any means through which the decision maker can resynthesize political and scientific factors into one policy. The varied political interests of a group may not be explicit in their public arguments. In fashioning a policy position that would stand a chance of being accepted, they may have suppressed certain political interests or exaggerated others. For example, in the New York City case, it is conceivable that the CBNS researchers opposed the waste-to-energy plant not because of the health risk posed by plant emissions *per se*, but because of their opposition to a waste management program that accepts uncritically the dominant concept of "waste." While actually working toward a public program aimed at solid waste reduction at the source rather than through so-called disposal technology, CBNS researchers might use the health risk argument to thwart the DOS proposal as a mobilizing strategy because the argument is more popularly embraced among the general citizenry (Schattschneider). Thus, although their opposition to the plant is articulated as contesting the imposition of an additional health risk on the population, their underlying political interest is to force a reevaluation of what they consider to be ecologically arrogant assumptions of the current system of industrial technology by eliminating options for waste disposal. Linking their opposition to the proposed facility to health reasons can be understood as a strategic ploy to appeal to the widest base of political support possible.

In such cases, the policy position presented to the decision maker does not necessarily include any sense of ranking of different issues or underlying concerns. Lacking this refinement, even a decision maker genuinely endeavoring to make a decision that meets the demands of various stakeholders would have great difficulty devising a decision that stakeholders view as fair or satisfying.

These methods also foster a hardening of policy positions. Through their investment of time, effort, and other resources in establishing a sound scientific and technical basis for a policy position, stakeholders become well-entrenched and firmly attached to their position. An agency, for example, must carefully document why a proposed action is needed and why it is environmentally and socially acceptable before announcing a proposal publicly. After an agency like EPA spends 3 to 5 years developing a set of rules that it believes are scientifically defensible and acceptable within its own bureaucratic structure, its "sunk costs" may become too great to allow staff to voluntarily consider modifications of any great magnitude. It would be difficult to imagine the Department of Sanitation deciding to forego its high technology waste treatment plans after more than 10 years of study. Through this time- and resource-consuming process, changes in policy alternatives become increasingly more difficult to justify in economic terms, and as the personal reputations of individuals involved are put on the line. For all parties, then, investment in supportive scientific or technical argumentation increases inflexibility on policy alternatives.

Finally, decision making methods that place an overemphasis on scientific and technical factors seriously distort public discourse by favoring policy alternatives that are substantiated by scientific argumentation. Distortion can affect the types of issues entered on the public agenda, and the types of parties who gain entry into the decision making arena. First, it will be more difficult for groups to promote policy positions whose scientific basis is not easily verifiable. In the anti-smoking campaign, for example, a group that might organize to oppose unrestricted cigarette smoking in public areas may not be taken seriously because of the difficulties in quantifying physical discomfort experienced from secondary smoke. In debates concerning the regulation of artificial sweeteners, the value of noncaloric sugar substitutes in reducing the health risk of obesity is a benefit purported by some proponents of artificial sweeteners. Again, however, measuring the reduction in the incidence or severity of obesity in the population that can be traced to the availability of artificial sweeteners is difficult, if not impossible. Again, the interests of such groups may be legitimate, but a process that places a premium on "technical wrappings" can not only foster, but condone their neglect. In short, concerns that are not easily quantified count less in the public decision making arena.

Second, screening out political claims not couched in technical phraseology discounts the concerns of affected parties who are unable to avail of appropriate expertise. Although a group is unable to formulate a scientific rationale for a preferred decision alternative, that policy alternative still may be technically feasible or their political interests may be met by another alternative that is scientifically sound. Groups may simply lack resources for analysis or access to expertise to enable them to "fully package" their positions.

Decision making procedures that fail to recognize the supremacy of political contests over scientific and technical aspects of public issues systematically disenfranchise large segments of the polity. Public decision making is distorted not only in terms of what kinds of issues are considered, but also in terms of who is allowed to speak and be heard.

The Role of the Scientist

Methods commonly used to resolve challenges to the scientific or technical basis of decision alternatives attempt to isolate the disputed scientific or technical points from the broader policy issues. The operating assumption underlying this approach is that issues of "fact" and "value," or "scientific fact" and "policy," are distinguishable. Conceptually congruent with the logical positivist empiricist view of science, expert committees are asked to rule on the "fact" portion of disputed public decisions. This division of "fact" and "values" creates a major dilemma for circumscribing the scientist's role and raises obstacles to democratic decision making.

First, although the membership of all committees is not rigidly prescribed, committees formed specifically to address disputed scientific points that bear on policy decisions are usually dominated, if not comprised exclusively, by technical specialists. Membership of the three committees comprising EPA's Science Advisory Board (SAB), for example, is required by statute to be

> a body of independent scientists and engineers of sufficient size and diversity to provide a range of expertise required to assess the scientific and technical aspects of environmental issues (Ashford: 75).

The tendency to appoint technically trained persons to advisory committees to rule on the "latest and best" information reflects, again, the presumption that an appropriate qualification for determining "best" is technical training. While a "range of expertise" is considered important, the representation of a range of political interests apparently is not. This reflects a presumption that different disciplinary training is an expected and acceptable cause for differing opinions, but different political interests and values among scientists are not.

The logical positivist empiricist view of science provides not only the theoretical basis for many conventional methods for managing scientific and technical information in public decision making, it also justifies a special place in decision making for the scientist. To the extent that determining the accuracy of contending scientific arguments contributes to the decision choice between two opposing policy alternatives, the role of the scientist is closer to one of arbiter of public policy. If the political allegiances of scientists are not made explicit and scientists are not accountable to the public, then questions about democratic decision making arise (Dickson).

The appointment of expert technical review committees also presents difficulties in terms of public credibility. In the debate preceding regulatory action to reduce airborne lead, for example, the National Academy of Sciences (NAS) prepared a report to guide the Environmental Protection Agency in standard-setting. The committee's findings were criticized for its failure to make definitive statements about the lead issue in contrast to the findings, one year later, by another group whose report based on essentially identical data was considerably more alarming. One writer noted that the NAS committee did not include any of the scientists whose work had initially flagged concern about the adverse health effects of airborne lead, although industry scientists were included (Boffey). Public awareness of such differences in "expert" findings and justifiable suspicions about the sympathies of members of such expert committees diminish the credibility of such efforts and their success in settling scientific disagreements.

Finally, conventional decision making methods that cultivate a highly antagonistic and competitive environment and set of relationships place scientists in a position that is contrary to the professed norms of the scientific community. In the ideal scientific community, individual scientists accept new data that support or contradict existing theories without prejudice. Mounting evidence contrary to existing theories presents scientists with an opportunity to develop new theories. In highly adversarial circumstances, however, in which scientific judgments are locked together with particular decision alternatives, scientists may feel reluctant to change their minds, especially if their employer or primary research funding source is a party to the dispute. Scientists thus cannot help but fall into sensitive and serious ethical dilemmas.

Economic ties notwithstanding, scientists are also often asked to make statements that they would not otherwise consider appropriate. While a scientist is comfortable stating the limitations of his ability to *know* a given fact, persons not trained in the natural sciences are sometimes intolerant of uncertainty. Decision makers and others attempting to influence the decision maker may press the scientist to make a determination between black and white when the scientific basis for doing so is lacking.

Summary

In this chapter, three hypothetical scenarios were presented in order to create a common reference point for a discussion of conventional public decision making and to illustrate common methods for handling scientific and technical information and disputes. Although these methods appear in slightly modified form in different institutional decision making contexts, they share many characteristics.

Conventional methods for resolving disagreement importantly share a theoretical foundation in logical positivist empiricism that constrains the ability of stakeholding groups to fully air either scientific or political arguments. Specifically, through these methods the basis of disagreement is obfuscated rather than clarified, the trust and credibility of stakeholders is forfeited, and political interests are left largely unacknowledged independently of positions substantiated by scientific arguments. As a result, since parties are often not satisfied, administrative decisions and decisions by elected officials are taken to court, often at least partially on the basis of disputed scientific premises. EPA was sued twice, once by a pro-environmental group and once by industry, before finally promulgating regulations to reduce airborne lead that stood. In both cases, science was an integral part of the legal challenges (*NRDC v. EPA*; *Ethyl v. EPA*). Legal decisions do not necessarily end disputes, however, since judicial rulings rarely reconcile contradictory scientific arguments and judgments and rulings that appear unfair and arbitrary to the losing party often are appealed in a higher court.

The value of destabilizing decisions should not be underestimated, however. Bouncing issues from one decision making forum to another serves a political purpose. Certain parties benefit by delaying action (Reisel; Susskind and Cruikshank). Preventing forward action on the Brooklyn Navy Yard mass-burn, waste-to-energy incinerator represented a positive gain to groups opposing the plant, such as the Williamsburg community, as long as their garbage continued to be collected by the city and taken away.

At some stage in many issues, however, changing circumstances may enhance the desirability of a more stable decision. If opposition groups perceived an impending waste management crisis in New York City, they might have a more favorable inclination toward a decision by the Board of Estimate, inasmuch as an outright rejection of the proposed facility would force the Department of Sanitation to more vigorously pursue other alternatives in order to clear the streets of a potential health hazard. In the wood stoves case, the traditional revulsion of industry to government regulation was assuaged by regulatory activity in several states. Throwing obstacles into EPA's rulemaking pathway might incite states that were already initiating regulatory action to move more quickly. Conversely, passage of federal regulations that appeared likely to be implemented would pacify state activity and prevent a multiplicity of state-level requirements on an industry doing interstate business. The party most likely to benefit by delaying an EPA rulemaking decision, in this case, was instead supportive.

The following chapter reconsiders the nature of scientific knowledge and presents an alternative approach for handling scientific and technical information in public decision making. These "consensus-based" methods are structurally more flexible than many conventional modes of soliciting public input. Importantly, they appear more consistent with a revised concept of the nature of "science" and how scientific knowledge can contribute to public decision making.

Notes

1. In a survey by Wenner of 1900 environmental lawsuits in the 1970s, 855 cases used NEPA as the primary law or to supplement other arguments.

2. The term "dioxin" is used to refer to two groups of closely related chemical compounds called polychlorinated dibenzo-p-dioxin (PCDD) and polychlorinated dibenzofuran (PCDF). The attack on mass-burn incinerators concerns the health risk posed by the two compounds combined.

3. The Environmental Protection Agency has since lowered its estimate of the toxicity of dioxin (see Note 13).

4. Stated by Barry Commoner during a personal interview, October 1986.

5. Telephone interview with Richard Colyer, May 1987.

6. One EPA staff person commented that he sees lobbyists more often than some of his colleagues during the preproposal stage of critical rules.

7. King (Colorado) suggested during telephone interview that his input into EPA's rulemaking effort would have been severely limited to simply submitting written comments on the proposed rule. Kowalczyk (Oregon) believed Oregon's participation would have also taken a formal path of submitting written comments on the proposed rule, but he also believed EPA would have been especially receptive to Oregon's input prior to formal rule proposal because of the state's leadership on this issue.

8. The standard of judicial review of agency adjudications and formal rulemaking proceedings is the more stringent "substantial evidence."

9. Hereforth referred to as the "Bays Mills tribe."

10. Hereforth referred to as "the Grand Traverse Band."

11. Stated by Special Master Francis McGovern during a telephone interview, August 1987.

12. *Legal Times*, April 22, 1985.

13. In 1988, the Environmental Protection Agency announced that it was downgrading its classification level of dioxin as "one of the most toxic subtances." The basis of this decision was allegedly findings of new studies that indicated toxicity levels much lower than previously believed. The new toxicity level assigned to dioxin by EPA, however, was not the level found by the new studies, but an arithmetic average between the new and old toxicity levels.

14. While in rare cases an academic researcher with no direct connections or even commonality of political interests with any particular stakeholder in a case may come forth as a friend of the court to introduce information to help clarify technical arguments for the court, I would argue that such cases are a very tiny minority. The U.S. in the final years of the 1980s is not an environment conducive to such altruistic actions. Even for willing souls, the demands of day-to-day life and professional survival often absorb completely an individual's energy and time allowances.

15. The selection of citizen advisory committees can vary substantially. In many cases, spokespersons for highly active environmental, residents, or business organizations are specially included. In other cases, appointment may be based on the official or unofficial status of community spokespersons, or simply the familiarity of agency personnel with such individuals. A primary concern of the sponsoring agency is that the committee appear credible (i.e., representative of the visible elements involved in the decision).

16. A record of such communications and their substantive content are added to the official, public record of the decision making procedure.

3

Consensus-Based Approaches to Handling Science

Foundations for Change

Conventional methods for soliciting scientific information and resolving disputed points in public decision making often leave those who choose to become involved frustrated and confused. Interest groups struggling to have their claims heard and addressed may feel shunted aside, their concerns ignored, or may feel they are listened to, but only after expending tremendous effort and financial resources. Decision makers may do their best to hear contending arguments, but may be at a loss when it comes to distinguishing between "good" science or flawed science, or making sense out of seemingly contradictory evidence. Confusion on scientific factors may even lead to the complete exclusion of technical considerations: a decision maker unable to understand critical scientific arguments may opt instead to react to the emotionalism of arguments. Disregarding technical parameters he believes are inconclusive anyway, he may choose to make a politically expedient decision, simply one that pleases a valued constituency.

Neither letting the science decide nor leaving the science out of decisions is desirable if decision making is to be both democratic and scientifically sound. There are alternatives to conventional methods for handling scientific information in public decision making, however. These procedures, grouped together roughly for their shared reliance on a consensus-based approach to dealing with scientific information, are promising because of the opportunities they offer stakeholders for expressing their political claims as well as contributing to the understanding of critical technical and scientific factors. Importantly, consensus-based approaches are theoretically compatible not with logical positivist empiricism, but with a "new" philosophy of science that has emerged over the past two decades. This "new" philosophy of science tolerates scientific disagreement, recognizes its political roots, and invites accommodation in decision making.

An Alternative Philosophy of Science

If the ideal of science, as depicted by the logical positivist empiricists could be met, public decision making would be simplified considerably. Debate would occur over the formulation and selection of policy alternatives (because of their unique distributive effects), but, as long as scientific endeavors were accepted as yielding one truth, a singular interpretation of reality, disputes over appropriate public actions would at least have a common starting point, as defined by technical constraints and considerations.

In fact, however, this ideal is not often met. Especially in work lying at the frontiers of knowledge, scientific efforts fail to answer many questions, partly because of the inherent difficulties with what Weinberg has called, "trans-scientific issues," and also because, as recent social studies by Albury, Mulkay, and others have argued, science is not monolithic.[1] The scientific method (including data collection, experimentation, and theory building), is performed within a web of value-bound assumptions and choices. Multiple branches of inquiry develop concurrently, sometimes ultimately converging on a common construction of reality, sometimes remaining at odds for extended periods of time. Consequently, scientific inquiry guarantees neither a singular way of knowing nor a solitary and absolute image of reality.

In contrast to logical positivist empiricism, an alternative philosophy of science acknowledges the social nature of scientific efforts and far greater degrees of ambiguity in scientific work. This "new philosophy of science," began to develop during the 1960s. Writers, such as Thomas Kuhn, pointed out the importance of paradigms, disciplinary lenses, and the "problem solving" nature of science. For example, Kuhn argued that scientists are trained, in a sense, indoctrinated, to accept a set of assumptions concerning models of theory and procedure. Even the determination of what constitutes a "fit" between plotted experimental data points and the curve suggested by a theoretical model is learned (Kuhn, 1982). Scientists work within this tightly constrained framework on "problems" until a given "paradigm" reaches a point of intellectual exhaustion and no longer provides a fruitful map for resolving unsettling questions (Ben-David). At such points, a "revolution" occurs, and a new theory or set of theories replaces the former (Kuhn, 1962). Scientific "truth" has a much more tentative ring in this context, being far more contingent on the conditions of observation and the theoretical framework within which the scientist works.

Science viewed this way, confers new meanings to disagreements among scientists. Differences may represent a turning point in a single line of scientific thought, (a "revolution" in Kuhn's language), or two alternative avenues for seeking truth, (distinct "paradigms" or "lenses" for viewing), rather than simply errors or faulty logic. Disagreements among scientists may represent alternative disciplinary training rather than incompetence.

Importantly, scientific disagreement in this framework does not necessarily indicate that one analysis is "correct" and another "incorrect," but rather represent two separate, both incomplete, "slices" of reality. That is, investigators may be examining different constellations of elements of a "system" or observing the same elements from significantly varied perspectives. These divergences may be particularly salient when questions lie at the frontier of existing knowledge.

Kuhn's seminal work coincided with a shift within the social studies of science. Other examinations of the activities of contemporary scientists suggest the influence of factors external to the laboratory on methodological choices made in the course of laboratory work (Latour; Knorr-Cetina). Such "external factors" affect the selection of research topics (Hubbard; Longino) and the communication of scientific work (Brooks; Mazur). These studies suggested that factors, such as personal experiential histories, employers and funding sources, and disciplinary tradition play key roles in shaping the products of scientific research, without contradicting the canons of the scientific method.

Technical Bases of Conflicting Scientific Advice

How do the characteristics of the investigator and the objectives of an investigation shape the findings of scientific research? Over the past twenty years, historians, philosophers and other social scientists have devoted considerable attention to understanding why scientists disagree and how divergent analysis can result from two equally "scientific" courses of investigation even within a single disciplinary tradition. Close examinations of what scientists do (e.g., laboratory experiment, analysis based on statistical data, or a review of existing reports), suggest that researchers repeatedly confront decision choices that are not strictly prescribed by their disciplinary training. The choice is mostly a function of personal judgment. Different judgments made at these critical junctures can produce notably dissimilar, even contradictory, research findings. The importance of personal judgment and discretionary decisions in various kinds of policy analysis (e.g., environmental impact assessment, risk assessment, cost-benefit analysis) has been noted by a number of authors (Bacow; Susskind and Dunlap), while others have performed similar analyses of laboratory conduct (Latour; Knorr-Cetina;).

Their findings suggest five reasons why scientists often proffer very different advice.[2]

Differences in research design include such steps as the framing of hypotheses, specification of assumptions (such as time frames, geographical boundaries, and functional definitions), and data selection (National Research Council; Mazur). The framing of hypotheses varies across different disciplines depending on the primary objectives and perspectives of the field. In predictive analysis, the specification of assumptions, especially the projection of future conditions, is critical. Even in laboratory science, the recording of data is dependent on functional definitions that may vary from one experiment to another, or from one laboratory to another. For example, the detection of "change" in a subject under study is dependent on the technology available for measuring change and the conventions used to define "change." In fields of rapid innovations in technological aids, similar experiments conducted over even a relatively short time interval may yield data in forms that are not comparable.

Differences in the interpretation of data or findings can arise in cases in which scientists may agree on a given piece of evidence, but disagree about its significance. In the anti-smoking policy debate, for example, some scientists viewed statistics on the association of lung cancer and smoking habits as a strong indication of a causal relationship. Others viewed the same statistics as supporting the hypothesis that lung cancer and smoking are both indications of a third condition, which is actually the causal factor inducing both disease and smoking in individuals. Interpretative differences arise from dissimilar choices of theory, or more directly, from contrary value orientations. Individuals who hold human health as the primary objective will often have a different calculus on interpretative issues from persons relatively more concerned with the stability of productive, economic activities, for example.

Confusing communication refers to the packaging of scientific information. Scientists, or the messengers who report scientific work, often employ rhetorical devices in their attempt to persuade decision makers and potential supporters of the policy implications of their scientific studies. For example, in the anti-smoking debate, one of the favorite phrases of tobacco supporters for many years was "there is no evidence to show that smoking causes lung cancer in humans." Technically speaking, this was true, since controlled experiments on humans were difficult to carry out because of ethical and other reasons, and the experiments on laboratory animals could be faulted for failing to accurately simulate human habits and living conditions.

Other confusing communication tactics include the representation of probabilities or statistical figures in ways which most favorably dramatize the numbers. For example, in the debate over nuclear weapons testing in the Pacific in the 1960s, scientists who supported testing expressed health dangers in terms of the increased chance of cancer for an individual exposed to fallout. The increased cancer risk to an individual appeared minute. In contrast, critics of testing expressed the same estimates in terms of actual deaths that would occur worldwide over a 50-year period as a result of expected fallout. These figures appeared very high (Brooks, 1980). Thus, while it appeared as though one analysis suggested a low health risk and the other a high risk, in fact, the estimates of likely increases in the incidence of human cancers cited by the two groups and the interpretation of these figures, were identical. For dramatic purposes, however, the scientists quite intentionally chose to express the risk estimates with different reference points (i.e., the individual in one case, the population in the other). The "disagreement" was, hence, purely attributable to differences in communication tactics.

Inappropriate policy prescriptions sometimes are surreptitiously inserted during the reporting of scientific information. Although a scientist may be asked solely to report on a particular "scientific" question concerning a given policy issue, the scientist may nonetheless include statements about his "personal" opinion, as the quote in Chapter 1 illustrated. As argued in Chapter 1, this distinction between "personal opinion," or values, and "scientific advice," or fact, is somewhat illusionary. While statements about policy prescriptions, in fact, simply reflect value orientations that are inherent in the advice anyway, the explicit statement of policy preference nonetheless further exacerbates the perception of disagreement among decision makers and others listening to the conflicting scientific testimony. Despite the fact that many decision alternatives may be consistent with a given identification of scientific and technical parameters, the expert voicing his own preference directs attention and, possibly, undue certification to that position.

Error remains a factor in the presentation of conflicting scientific information in public decision making (Wessel). While no studies indicate the degree to which error accounts for debate, it is conceivable that some scientists may retract opinions after additional data that brings into questions their earlier assumptions becomes available. Finally, a closely related issue, and one that has gained notice in recent years, is the outright falsification of data and research in the scientific community. Alternative views of the scientific enterprise and the nature of scientific disagreement have profound implications for the use of science in public decision making. If conflicting scientific evidence or analyses are considered legitimate from a scientific perspective, understanding the value choices that lead one investigator to one conclusion and another to a different conclusion from a similar starting point is critical to a decision maker (and others) wishing to assess the compatibility of competing scientific arguments with her own values and policy choices. Rather than simply dismissing science as "not useful" in informing policy decisions when experts disagree, decision makers are faced with the challenge of devising decisions that address multiple estimates of reality, or of explaining why they accept one version and not others. Moreover, if scientists are not politically neutral and dispassionate, then scientific analysis and the advice of scientists can not be held up as authoritative in public decision making without obfuscating the underlying political conflicts and usurping political power.

Can public decision making procedures be adjusted to account for the biases of the scientist when scientific information, particularly contradictory analyses, is presented? If decision makers and other non-scientists could decipher why scientists submit conflicting testimony, would they be better equipped to comprehend the value orientations embodied in each analysis or report? Would a recognition of the vulnerability of scientific work to politics and values clear the path for a more straightforward discussion of the interests and values at stake in the decision? In short, can procedures be instigated to defuse the disruptive and destructive effects of scientific disagreement in public debates?

Consensus-Based Methods for Science-Intensive Public Decisions

Many writers have speculated on the theoretical compatibility of consensus-based procedures, such as negotiation and mediation, with science-intensive public disputes. They have cited such techniques as joint fact-finding or data collection, collaborative model building, and the assistance of an intervenor,[3] and the flexible structure as particular features of consensus-based methods that are likely to contribute to less adversarial uses of scientific information, greater opportunities for understanding the basis of disagreements, and higher probabilities of reaching an agreement on technical issues intimately linked to public decisions. They contend that constructing a common understanding of technical points contributes to an environment in which participants can then debate more explicitly political decisions (Bacow and Wheeler; Cormick and Knaster; Susskind and McCreary).

In fact, the actual applications of consensus-based methods in public decision making up to the present has varied considerably, complicating efforts to perform a systematic study of the impact of these methods on public decision making. Many of the 160 cases of consensus-based interventions in environmental disputes between 1973–1983 in the United States occurred outside of conventional, institutionalized proceedings. The *ad hoc* nature of negotiation and mediation efforts in public disputes, together with differences on a multitude of potentially significant dimensions such as the nature of the dispute, its intensity, the specific interests and resources of stakeholding parties, their incentives to resolve the dispute, relationships among parties, particular techniques employed, and characteristics and objectives of the intervenor further complicates an assessment of the efficacy of consensus-based approaches to resolving science-intensive public disputes.

The apparent consistency of consensus-based approaches with a view of science that tolerates uncertainty and disagreement creates a powerful urge to explore further the relationship between these methods and science-intensive public disputes, however. The overriding question is, do consensus-based procedures affect the role of science in public disputes in any consistent or predictable pattern or direction? One step toward answering this question is a close examination of how consensus-based procedures affected the role of science in actual cases.

Three Procedures for Science-Intensive Decision Making

Referring again to the the three cases used hypothetically in the previous chapter on conventional decision making, we turn now to look at how consensus-based procedures were actually applied in each of these decision making scenarios. These three examples illustrate how consensus-based methods offer alternative ways of handling scientific and technical information and disputes. The cases suggest three distinct procedures: One case shows how understanding the causes of scientific disagreement can move decision making forward; another shows how building a consensus on technical aspects of a decision can lead to agreement on policy; the third case portrays a procedure for reaching a policy agreement in the presence of substantial technical uncertainty. Importantly, in all three cases, the procedures permitted a far greater degree of flexibility in dealing with technical and political uncertainty, as compared to the conventional "decide-announce-defend" approach.

Procedure 1: Understanding the Basis of Scientific Disagreement

The New York Academy of Sciences facilitated policy dialogue represents a rather narrow form of intervention. The objective, as described by Don Straus, chair of the Science and Society Committee of the Academy, was not "to solve or even suggest solutions to how to solve waste disposal" but to "help representatives of the BOE to walk through scientific issues concerned with how to solve solid waste disposal" (New York Academy of Sciences, 1984b). In fact, even this seemingly limited objective overstates the actual accomplishment of the 8-hour, one-day session. The achievement was modest: simply to trace the basis for the discrepant risk assessments performed in respect to one solid waste management option, namely the proposed Brooklyn Navy Yard facility. Nonetheless, even this relatively minor accomplishment might not have occurred without a consensus-based procedure.

A Close Look at the Scientific Disagreement. The New York Academy of Sciences policy dialogue was undertaken in response to an urgent plea for assistance from the New York City Department of Sanitation (Konkel). One month after the Department of Sanitation (DOS) announced its plan to construct a resource recovery facility at the Brooklyn Navy Yard site, the Center for the Biology of Natural Systems (CBNS) issued the first of four reports condemning the project for exposing the City's residents to an increased risk of developing cancer. The city's governing Board of Estimate (BOE) instructed the DOS to conduct further study, which was embodied in a report by Fred C. Hart and Associates, Inc. Under what each called a "worst-case" scenario, the Hart report estimated an increase of 5.9 cancer cases per 1 million population exposed over a 70-year lifetime while the CBNS report predicted a range of 29 to 1,430 additional cases of cancer per million population (Commoner, 1984).

What accounted for this startling, 240-fold discrepancy? Briefly, the different figures can be traced to differing opinions on two main factors: (1) predicted dioxin emission levels, and (2) the effectiveness of proposed pollution control technologies. These two factors, in turn, are inextricably bound to a theory of the mechanisms of dioxin formation in municipal solid waste (MSW) incinerators.

Differing assumptions about the level of dioxin emissions is the singular risk assessment variable that goes the furthest in explaining why the two cancer risk assessments differed by more than a factor of 240. If the same expected emission level is factored into each analysis, the Hart and CBNS risk analyses respectively yield values of 5.9 and 29 additional cancer cases per 1 million population exposed over a 70-year lifetime. Given the high level of uncertainty in this type of risk assessment, a less than 5-fold difference between projections is not a significant variation (Commoner, 1984: IV-18).

Estimating expected levels of dioxin emissions is an imprecise task. Although reports on dioxin emissions from municipal incinerators appeared in the mid-1970s from the works of European researchers, existing data in 1984 was still spotty, idiosyncratic, and, as a result, inconclusive. The Hart report identified data on dioxin emissions from 19 incinerators located around the world. However, monitoring protocols, the specific identity of the dioxin isomers tested, the physical state of the dioxin compounds tested, and numerous other methodological details for each of these tests varied, making the comparability of performances among these existing facilities difficult to judge. Moreover, separating valid from invalid testing results was impossible.

The different research groups took different approaches to selecting an appropriate emission estimate for their risk analyses. From those 19 sets of emissions test data listed in the appendices of the Hart report, authors of the Hart report combined two sets of testing data, from the Chicago Northwest and the Zurich-Josefstrasse facilities for their risk assessment. They justified their selective use of data on the basis of similarities between the proposed BNY facility and these two facilities with respect to furnace design, location (ie., in a large U.S. metropolitan area), and waste composition and on the basis of sampling methodology (Hart: 3-19, 3-20). Interestingly, as the authors themselves note, emissions data from these two facilities were also among the lowest reported (Hart: 3-15).

The key words in the Hart report are "data selected as the most representative." In contrast, CBNS researchers looked at the available data comprehensively, rather than exclusively. They interpreted the wide range of test results as indicating the high variability and unpredictable nature of dioxin emissions, rather than as resulting from the varying reliability of measurement techniques in different cases. They asserted that too little is understood about the dynamics of dioxin emissions to confidently judge representativeness and comparability between plants. To safeguard against such gaps in knowledge, the CBNS analysts utilized both the lowest and the highest tested emission levels in their risk assessment, (thereby yielding a range of expected increases in cancer rates, from 29 to 1,430 additional cases), without attempting to judge their relative validity (Commoner, 1984: I-9, 10).

In subsequent reports, the CBNS research team continued to refute reasons offered by the Hart group for justifying their more narrow data selection. In particular, the CBNS analysts contested the relevance of design similarities cited by the Hart group as justification for their data selection. They argued that the Chicago, Northwest and Zurich-Josefstrasse facilities are more similar to the proposed BNY plant than the other facilities for which testing data were relatively complete, only in that they utilize a Martin grate (part of the furnace system). Other potentially important features such as the size of the facility were not similar. Moreover, they contested the role of the Martin grate and furnace operating conditions in affecting dioxin levels. They cited recent testing data from a Tsushima, Japan incinerator equipped with a Martin grate, which showed emission levels ten times higher than the Chicago, Northwest test data despite furnace temperatures of 800 degrees centigrade (Commoner, 1984) and a Canadian study which indicated that emission rates were not significantly affected by temperature or other combustion factors (Commoner, 1984: IV-10).

At the core of the disagreement over the appropriate data set and the significance of the furnace system were assumptions about the formation and destruction of dioxin in MSW incinerators. There was no challenge to the proposition that dioxins are destroyed at very high temperatures (800 degrees centigrade or higher). It was uncontested that under optimum conditions of air turbulence, oxygen concentration, residence time, and high temperatures, laboratory experiments have shown about 99 percent of dioxins present are destroyed. It was also more or less undisputed that the furnace design proposed for the BNY plant would be capable of destroying a significant proportion of the dioxin in the combustion chamber, although there certainly was room for disagreement on this issue.

What was contested was whether dioxin is actually present in the combustion chamber at all. The formation of dioxin in incinerators is not well understood. In their effort to knit together the pieces of information obtained through past studies, researchers developed three alternative hypotheses to explain dioxin formation. The first is that dioxin compounds are present in the raw refuse and are volatized during incineration. Since PCDDs and PCDFs are known to have formed as byproducts and contaminants of commercial chemical goods commonly found in municipal refuse (such as polychlorinated biphenyls [PCBs]), it is reasonable to assume that municipal wastes may contain traces of dioxin. In fact, one study did detect PCDFs and PCDDs in raw wastes, although not in sufficient quantities to explain tested dioxin emission levels (given the generally accepted fact that laboratory experiments have demonstrated that about 99% of the dioxins present are destroyed at high temperatures.)

The second hypothesis, one regarded as the conventional theory, posits that PCDDs and PCDFs are formed from precursors present in the waste stream. Precursors are products (such as PCBs and chlorophenols) that contain PCDF and PCDD materials as contaminants. It is hypothesized that PCDFs and PCDDs form at temperatures sufficient to decompose precursors but too low to destroy dioxin. PCDFs and PCDDs can also volatize directly from precursor materials. Laboratory experiments have provided data consistent with this theory, although no studies have yielded conclusive data (Hart: 3-4). In fact, one experiment indicated that adding precursor materials to the waste stream did not significantly increase the PCDF and PCDD concentrations found adsorbed onto fly ash (Hart: 3-5).

The third theory proposes that PCDDs and PCDFs are synthesized *de novo* from constituents of materials commonly present in the waste stream, such as wood products and plastics. The "*de novo* synthesis" theory of the formation of dioxin has been deduced from laboratory experiments that have shown that no dioxin is emitted when certain materials are burned separately but is detected when these and related products are incinerated together. According to this theory, PCDDs and PCDFs are formed in municipal solid waste (MSW) incinerator systems by chemical reactions between carbon-ring compounds produced by the incomplete combustion of lignin (a constituent of wood and paper), and chlorine in the form of hydrochloric acid. Hydrochloric acid is produced in incinerators by the combustion of chlorine-containing plastics (such as polyvinyl chloride, or "vinyl") that are present in MSW and ordinary table salt, which provides an unknown, but apparently minor, contribution. Paper is the major source of lignin in MSW (Center for the Biology of Natural Systems: IV-8).

Distinct from the preceding two theories, the *de novo* synthesis theory further posits that syntheses of PCDDs and PCDFs do not occur in the incinerator, but at later points in the waste gas stream. The carbon-ring compounds and chlorine compounds are freed from their original state during the combustion process and adsorb onto particles of fly ash. These constituents of PCDDs and PCDFs then react under lower temperatures (in the smokestack or other points beyond the combustion chambers) to form PCDDs and PCDFs. As in the case of the conventional theory, the results of at least one experiment appear to contradict this theory (Hart: 3-5).

The authors of the Hart report acknowledged the ambiguity of existing empirical evidence by recognizing that dioxin formation may occur by more than one mechanism. They argued, however, that the 10-degree design temperature difference between the pollution control device and the stack of the proposed facility made condensation in the stack unlikely and that PCDF and PCDD materials adsorbed before entering the pollution control device would be trapped in the fabric filter (Hart: 3-23). Implicitly, they justified a narrow data set on the assumption that dioxin is present in the raw waste or is formed from precursors during the combustion step and can be destroyed under optimum heat conditions. They further assumed that any dioxin formed subsequent to the high temperature chambers is likely to form before, not in, the stack, and will therefore be contained by the fabric filter control system.

The CBNS team more adamantly subscribed to only one theory, the *de novo* synthesis theory. In their report they described tests from the Tsushima, Japan incinerator, which is similar to the proposed plant in furnace design and equipped with the same pollution control system. They claimed that tests showed that this system failed to control PCDD/PCDF emissions and that PCDDs and PCDFs were, in fact, synthesized in the control system with seven times as much PCDD/PCDF leaving the control system (emitted through the stack) as entered it (CBNS: IV-11).

The relevance of the process of dioxin formation to the BNY proposal is two-fold. First, if PCDDs and PCDFs are indeed formed by precursors in the waste stream as the conventional theory holds, then they ought to be destroyed if appropriate incineration conditions are maintained. On the other hand, if the *de novo* synthesis theory is true, and synthesis occurs only after temperatures in the waste gas stream are sufficiently cooled, then PCDDs and PCDFs would not be present in the combustion process at all and high incineration temperatures and other combustion factors such as air turbulence and oxygen balance could be expected to have no effect on emission levels. Thus, if the conventional theory is true, the importance of the Martin grate in selecting emission level data is substantiated and a lower risk estimate may be more accurate. Conversely, if the *de novo* synthesis theory is correct, this design feature would be arguably less significant in relation to data selection, and a higher risk estimate is warranted.

Theories of dioxin formation also have implications for evaluating the effectiveness of pollution control technologies. If PCDD and PCDF precursors are present as contaminants in single products, waste separation before incineration would have no effect on dioxin emission levels. If formation occurs during combustion, then increasing the effectiveness of particulate emission control systems should reduce dioxin emissions. If dioxin is formed in accordance with the *de novo* synthesis theory, "add-on" air pollution control technologies would be useless unless a significant proportion of the dioxin formation occurred before or in the control technology system. In that case, waste separation prior to incineration would appear much more promising to reduce emissions.

This account of the New York City dispute shows that discrepancies in the work of reputable scientists can occur when the scientists hold differing opinions about factors that cannot be ascertained given the present state of knowledge. These two groups of researchers reached different determinations on the appropriate data set largely because of the lack of conclusive information on the mechanism of dioxin formation in MSW incinerators. The absence of definitive theory, together with contradictory test results from dissimilar facilities obtained under unquantifiably varying conditions and findings from laboratory studies whose extrapolation to real world experiences is questionable, enabled each to construct equally plausible and persuasive scientific rationales for critically different data selections.

Without knowing the relative impact of various factors on dioxin emissions, some scientists are willing to make assumptions where others are not. Without conclusive evidence to support one theory of dioxin formation over another, scientists may intuitively find one argument more compelling than another. The willingness to make assumptions, the "intuition" that attracts an individual to one theory over others, like personal "risk aversity" levels, are intermediate manifestations of the individual's unique set of values, experiential history, and position within the current debate. When disagreement surfaces, the controversy may heat up to the point that groups intentionally (or not) engage in communicative manipulations, such as using single terms like "worst case" to convey different meanings.

These kinds of disagreements arise again and again in science-intensive public disputes, in varied renditions, as the latter two cases illustrate. In what ways did the facilitated policy dialogue function to enlighten the decision makers (in this case, their staff advisors) on the issue of dioxin emissions and solid waste incinerators?

Decoding Scientific Disagreements. The "by-invitation-only" facilitated policy dialogue was set up as a one-day session to address three specific issues concerning the proposed mass-burn incinerator (New York Academy of Sciences, 1984a). The three issues, which were selected by staff from the New York Academy of Sciences after consultation with members of the BOE, included: (1) the types of emissions and their health effects, (2) the sources of emissions in resource recovery plants, and (3) the control of emissions. After 30-minute presentations on each topic from expert panelists, who were also selected by the Academy staff in consultation with BOE staff and representatives of major environmental groups, the floor was opened to questions from other panelists, BOE staff, and the general audience.

The isolated opportunity that the one-day session offered scientists to present their views made the occasion vulnerable to attempts at "grandstanding." In some cases, presenters used the forum to defend their opinions and interpretations of study results. For example, one panelist, a chemist whose work had been cited in CBNS reports, was asked to address the issue of the sources of PCDD and PCDF emissions from mass-burn plants. He spent much of his 15 minutes rendering a carefully prepared statement condemning the "CBNS theory" (the *de novo* theory) and clarifying what he believed was the proper interpretation of the results of his research. His reinterpretation of historical data cited by CBNS provoked a strong rebuttal by Commoner during the following question and answer period. This interval of the policy dialogue, which can be characterized as highly antagonistic, seemed to constitute little more than an opportunity for the speakers to present orally their own "adventures in applied probability."[4]

In contrast, the question and answer period in other instances helped to clarify exactly what the experts, in their cautious, scientific language rich with disclaimers, were actually saying. The dialogue allowed the audience an opportunity to gain an appreciation of the contingent nature of what could be viewed as prescriptive advice (such as an estimate of the effectiveness of emission reduction technologies) and descriptive scientific theory (such as assumptions about the formation and destruction of dioxins). The mediator assisted in these interactions between decision maker representatives and experts by rephrasing questions and responses, and by reminding speakers of the focus of the discussion. In some cases, the mediator's attempt to rephrase a question helped the asker to express it more clearly himself. In other cases, the mediator's attempt to repeat a response was corrected by the respondent. All of these efforts helped to clarify the scientist's view for the non-scientist listener.

Perhaps most importantly, what was achieved was not only merely the disclosure of the technical basis for differing risk assessments, but the disengagement of two polar opposite policy positions—to build and not to build the plant—from the scientific issues. The lay-out of the issues, the question-and-answer format, and the mediator's vigilance helped to keep clear the distinction between what is known about dioxin formation and destruction and pollution control technologies, and the desirability of different technologies. Rather than a "black and white" choice between a plant with high emissions and no plant and no emissions, a richer landscape of alternatives was drawn as individuals became inspired to suggest novel ways of dealing with uncertainty. One suggestion heard was to require the builders of the mass-burn incinerator to bear the costs incurred if a plant is shut down for failure to attain agreed on emission levels, for example. This is an intriguing way to force those most confident of their assertions to gamble the hardest.

It is also significant that Dr. Barry Commoner, the leading scientist-spokesperson opposing the proposed Brooklyn Navy Yard facility and a participant at the facilitated policy dialogue, sent a letter that was published in the *New York Times* three days after the meeting. Reasserting his belief that DOS estimates of dioxin emissions were inaccurately understated, he proposed that a "good way to cut through the controversy, which was suggested by a recent action by California in response to an incinerator issue" (and a suggestion that was raised at the NYAS policy dialogue) was to require "the builder to show, by tests on the completed incinerator, that it does, in fact, emit dioxin at the low rate that the builder predicts" (*New York Times*, January 5, 1985). This statement by Commoner seems to indicate that the two issues—the question of the cancer risk posed by dioxin emissions from the proposed facility and the question of whether to build the facility or not—were successfully severed by the discussions at the policy dialogue.

One Step Toward Decision. The New York City Board of Estimate voted to approve the comprehensive waste management plan on December 20 1984, only two days after the policy dialogue (*New York Times*, December 21, 1984). Public opposition to the high-tech waste management plan persisted, but in August 1985, the BOE approved the Brooklyn Navy Yard proposal as well (*New York Times*, August 16, 1985). In response, members of the Williamsburg community organized a mass protest march to City Hall and a spokesperson was quoted as saying, "We will be at the site every single day, a single bulldozer will not enter that site" (*New York Times*, September 6, 1985). Residents subsequently filed legal suit and construction of the plant has been delayed indefinitely.

Disengaging decision alternatives from disputes over scientific or technical issues is only the first step in developing a politically acceptable decision. The facilitated policy dialogue was not designed to take the discussion beyond the point of clarifying disagreements between experts. Consequently, although potentially it reopened the discussion to new alternatives and the expression of political interests, the policy dialogue was not directed toward facilitating either process. It presented opportunities, but without strong inducements for action.

The decision alternatives that were added to the discussion partly as a result of the information that surfaced at the policy dialogue consisted of add-on air pollution control technologies and more stringent monitoring provisions to ensure expected operating conditions are not violated. One might argue also that advocates of alternatives to mass-burn incineration gained political ground since legitimization of the higher risk assessment and the *de novo* theory of dioxin formation would have made recycling and other approaches appear more appealing to decision makers hoping to allay public fears. While the actual benefits to advocates of alternative waste processing methods afforded by the policy dialogue are difficult to identify absolutely, it certainly is plausible that the policy dialogue broadened the consideration of decision alternatives to include ones more compatible with the political objectives of these groups.

On the other hand, the relatively limited scope of the policy dialogue, in terms of objectives and scheduling, did not allow for more revealing discussions of political interests. The meeting was focussed entirely on scientific issues. Although this was useful in disclosing some value choices behind divergent technical analyses, (e.g., how conservative a stance to assume in estimating variables), it did not flush out statements about the motivations of various groups involved.

For some groups, the political interests that spurred action were less clear than those of others. Although the CBNS researchers and the Williamsburg community sat on the same side in the scientific dispute, the political interests behind their involvement were probably quite distinct. The Williamsburg residents opposed the Brooklyn Navy Yard plant because it was slotted for a site adjacent to their neighborhood. Although general public health risks were certainly of concern to them, it is not clear that they would have spoken out against a similar plant had it been proposed for a location elsewhere in Brooklyn, in the Bronx, or in another state.

The motivation of the CBNS researchers can be surmised quite differently. Dr. Commoner has been part of public opposition to mass-burn incinerators in several communities outside his own. From his extensive writings, his involvement and those of his colleagues at CBNS might be understood as a manifestation of a commitment toward restructuring a "wasteful," environmentally assaultive society into a more ecologically balanced one.[5] The fact that Dr. Commoner advocated recycling, waste sorting, and source reduction in lieu of mass-burn incineration reinforces this interpretation of Dr. Commoner's motives. On the other hand, his involvement may simply be motivated by a belief in self-determination and a response to a request for assistance from a community struggling to gain control of its future.[6] In any case, his political motives were probably broader and more ideologically oriented than those of the Williamsburg community.

The interests of other groups present at the policy dialogue can be expected to differ again from these two groups. However, the policy dialogue did not encourage a discussion of the concerns and interests behind the involvement of various groups. Consequently, it provided little additional enlightenment to decision makers aiming to make a politically acceptable and technically reasonable decision.

Procedure 2: Building a Technical Consensus[7]

The woodburning stoves regulatory negotiation was a fairly comprehensive attempt to weave technical and scientific knowledge into the policy making trade-offs necessary in developing implementable technology-based pollution control regulations. In contrast to the facilitated policy dialogue and the Michigan fishing case, the regulatory negotiation preceded any well-publicized debate over the issue under consideration, emission standards for new residential wood combustion units. The participants held a wide range of concerns and were variously equipped to deal with scientific, legal, and regulatory aspects of rulemaking.

Putting the Process in Motion. The Environmental Protection Agency's objective was to develop rules that were politically palatable, enforceable, and technically feasible. EPA had previous experience with the use of negotiation in rulemaking. The agency, through its Office of Program Planning and Evaluation, had undertaken a pilot project in regulatory negotiation beginning in 1983 and by mid-1985, three of the six demonstration "reg negs" were completed or underway (Harter, 1986). The EPA process designers, through consultation with the Standards Development Branch, were also familiar with the nature and type of issues that would require consideration in the wood stoves case, and the critical limitations of the technical and scientific knowledge needed to back up decisions. Although regulations agreed upon by the negotiating parties were preferable, even without signatures, EPA would be closer to promulgating appropriate rules at the end of the negotiation effort since much of the technical and policy issues would be clarified through the discussions.

By early 1986, the Standards and Development Branch of EPA sent letters to about 20 prospective participants announcing the Agency's intention to undertake a regulatory negotiation process and inviting recipients to attend the first organizational meeting. The agency also issued a notice in the February 7, 1986 *Federal Register* informing and inviting the wider public to indicate their interest by attending the first meeting. Included in this public notice was a description of the procedure for identifying participants in the regulatory negotiation. EPA states,

> We do not believe that each potentially affected organizational [sic] or individual must necessarily have its own representative. However, we firmly believe that

each interest must be adequately represented. Moreover, we must be satisfied that the group as a whole reflects a proper balance and mix of interests (*Federal Register*, 1986).

Fifteen individuals representing an array of interests,[8] plus the EPA negotiator were officially designated the negotiating group. Most of the members were among the original list of EPA invitees; two additional members successfully argued for a seat at the negotiating table at the first meeting and were accepted by consensus of the group overall.

An EPA staff person initially intended to serve as mediator, but the EPA-hired consultant, originally acting as "convener" quickly took over all facilitating as well as convening responsibilities in response to requests by the participants. The negotiations were structured around six two- and three-day meetings that took place at regular intervals over a period of six months. Meetings were announced in the *Federal Register* and open to the public. Observers were were encouraged to ask questions and submit additional information and comments to the negotiating group upon procedural recognition from the facilitator. Discussions were often lengthy, but rich with the engineering, legal, and regulatory knowledge of many individuals as well as intense debate between parties with competing interests.

As in the New York City waste processing plant dispute, the science and technology of wood stoves is not well understood. Emissions vary in accordance with a number of difficult-to-control factors, including user habits, such as the way one stacks wood, wood type and age, burn rates, and other such variables, as well as differences in stove design. Although stoves equipped with catalysts are widely believed to burn more "cleanly," a lack of long-term data arouses doubt about the overall performance of catalysts in reducing emission levels. Moreover, it is suspected that catalysts degrade through use, but how quickly degradation occurs and the effect of alternative catalyst materials and stove designs on degradation rates is not known. Finally, the difference between emission levels occurring during laboratory testing and actual home-use is also highly speculative.

The level of technical ambiguity surrounding wood stove emissions opened the door for analytical acrobatics and political posturing by the stakeholding parties. Instead, through the negotiations the parties apparently recognized the uncertain nature of the calculations over which they labored. Sometimes, through an iterative process, agreement would be reached on one number or one method of measurement or analysis. More often, a sort of "bounded" ambiguity prevailed. In these cases, the negotiations over "hard numbers," such as permissible emission levels, compliance dates, and so on, transpired in a climate in which negotiators had a common acceptance of the range of scientifically acceptable estimations. In determining the package of provisions that comprised the ultimate regulations, negotiators traded across issues (sometimes called "logrolling" in the negotiation literature),[9] accepting higher estimates on one variable that justified one party's preferred policy choice, in exchange for lower estimates on another variable which supported another party's preference on a different provision. What resulted was a mosaic of rules and regulations which has not been seriously criticized after publication and which most parties believe are as scientifically and technically sound as possible to develop under the prevailing time constraints.

Reaching a Technical Consensus. This scientific and technical consensus was accomplished in a number of different ways. Although EPA staff persons had appropriate technical training which was supplemented by hired consultants, the accelerated rulemaking schedule resulting from the NRDC lawsuit settlement meant that the agency would be hard pressed to generate independent scientific and technical data. By involving many parties in the rulemaking process, some of the effort and cost of gathering data were, in effect, "externalized." The negotiating parties, notably the WHA, the independent testing laboratories, and the states of Oregon and Colorado, which have operational regulatory programs, volunteered data and technical analysis on issues of their particular concern as well as in response to requests by others during meetings. As a result, the regulatory negotiation format allowed the group to assemble a massive amount of existing information rapidly in usable form.

Data and analysis presented by parties with a strong interest in a particular decision are often looked upon skeptically by the receivers—be they decision makers, other interested parties, or observers—and with good reason. While industry is commonly accused of underestimating health risks associated with the use of chemical substances in the workplace (Marcus) and overestimating the costs of proposed regulations, government has been found to exaggerate the benefits of proposed regulations (Brownstein). Hence, information contributed by parties with a strong stake in a decision is often viewed as biased, incomplete, or even inaccurate. In the regulatory negotiation setting, negotiators, their expert advisors, and observers were able to freely question the party presenting the information about data sources, assumptions of the methodology, and others details of research design. When EPA presented an econometric model to predict the impact of exempting small manufacturers from the regulations, for example, skeptical negotiators were invited to submit alternative input values, or assumptions, to yield predictions under varying conditions.

Error in data or analysis could be detected as group members carefully scrutinized each item submitted. Even if no flaws or inconsistencies were uncovered in the cross-examination, the listeners, experts and non-experts alike, gained a sense of the data's validity, an understanding of the underlying assumptions of the analysis, and general significance of the information simply by the tenor of the discussion.[10] With the stakeholders physically together, technical arguments were "on trial" to be judged by the group as a whole, not only by EPA. Overall, the credibility of data and analyses subjected to careful, open, and interactive viewing in this way was increased significantly.[11]

The structure of the negotiation sessions also allowed for the presentation of contradictory, inconsistent, and complementary scientific and technical evidence and arguments in a way that maximized the opportunity for understanding how and why they differ. When technical disagreements and uncertainties seemed too unwieldy for the mixed group to handle, subcommittees formed (comprising representatives from each major coalition) to examine the issue more closely and come back to the larger group with some kind of clarification, if not a consensus. Because the negotiations were structured so that all issues were introduced in the earlier sessions and then "revisited" during the later meetings of final deliberations and bargaining, participants also had an opportunity to seek independent reviews and consultations (US EPA, 1984) and to submit additional materials for consideration by the group through mailings and over the wires. Thus, a considerable amount of debate over the technical aspects occurred, allowing a full airing of multiple sides of the issues (alternative interpretation, inconsistent data, competing theories, etc.).

Also, as in the NYAS policy dialogue, the participation of both "expert" and "non-experts" in a variety of specialized fields forced individuals to maintain a language that was relatively clean of jargon, rhetoric, and deceptive manipulations. In addition to the fact that many participants indicated that they were not shy about demanding clarification on points even at the risk of revealing their ignorance, the facilitator also made deliberate efforts to pull in the reins on any speaker who rambled on in technical jargon or without clear explanations. It is interesting to note that despite conspicuous efforts to keep the discussions comprehensible to all participants, inevitably certain topics were overly complex for everyone to follow. Surprisingly, however, individuals who later admitted the discussions sometimes went over their heads, claimed that they did not feel they had been "snowed." Their confidence in the strength of the bonding among members of their coalition apparently provided sufficient reassurance that if their interests were threatened by any of the discussions, coalition members more competent on the technical aspects of the case would alert them accordingly.[12]

It seemed that the participants were satisfied at the end of the negotiations with the scientific validity and technical feasibility of the rules they collaborated in writing. Participants commented that political positions (policy options) were always grounded in what was technically possible. The inclusion of technically expert persons in each major coalition meant that individuals with a particular concern could thrash it out during a caucus and the coalition members together could develop a technically-sound proposal to suggest to the larger negotiating group.

Although there seems to have been a considerable amount of give-and-take during this regulatory negotiation including a substantial amount of information sharing and debate over methodological assumptions and technical ambiguities, many participants also noted that they did not believe that EPA had relinquished any real control over the rulemaking procedure. A number of participants commented that, throughout the negotiations, EPA seemed to draw certain lines over which they would not cross, regardless of the technical or political arguments proffered.[13] One person interviewed described the lead EPA negotiator's attitude on particular issues as being one of "Don't confuse me with the facts." In other words, the respondents indicated a certain close-mindedness on the part of the EPA in regard to hearing scientific or technical arguments in support of positions the agency (apparently for political reasons) was not prepared to back. Negotiators seemed not seriously discouraged by EPA's behavior, however, and instead showed a sort of appreciation of the agency's own bureaucratic and political tightrope (constraints resulting from provisions such as the Office of Management and Budget's oversight role in rulemaking, which is to assess the economic impact of proposed rules as required under Executive Order 12991).

Managing Science to Forge a Political Consensus. The consensus-based procedure employed in the EPA rulemaking negotiation was a comprehensive and deliberate attempt by EPA to orchestrate the submission of technical information and the expression of political interests. While the agency retained a considerable degree of control over the process through its success at unilaterally invoking limits to discussions and, at times, refusing to entertain further technical arguments, negotiators nonetheless expressed a sense of participation in decision making unusual under conventional proceedings. Discussions on relevant scientific and technical points were adversarial and competitive, but not destructive or unproductive.

Three factors contributed to this treatment of scientific and technical components of the rule's development. First, although negotiators freely submitted technical information and analysis in a way that might have explicitly supported or challenged certain policy alternatives, the discussion format of the negotiations provided opportunities for ample questioning and clarification. As in the NYAS policy dialogue, participants developed a more thorough understanding of the basis for differences in data and analyses and a mutual appreciation of the uncertain nature of both the scientific and technical premises and the actual effects of various regulatory actions. Importantly, both scientific and regulatory "uncertainty" were accepted as facts of life given the current state of knowledge and as the necessary basis for policy rather than as an opportunity for casting doubt on the desirability and suitability of a proposed action.

Second, the timing of the consensus-based intervention was significant. Since the negotiations occurred prior to a complete formulation of the rule by any party, participants did not begin the procedure reacting against certain options. That is, because more or less the entire rule was yet to be developed, participants recognized the contingent nature of their initial positions on various provisions of the rule and refrained from explicitly ranking policy options, rather viewing the issues as a package. A stricter emission standard would be more reasonable from the manufacturers' perspective if the compliance date was coordinated to coincide with production cycles so that design changes could be made without interruption in production, for example. In contrast, if manufacturers instead had been presented with a fully formulated rule proposed by EPA, they would have likely launched an attack on the scientific merits or technical feasibility of the numerical standards rather than suggest adjustments to other portions of the rule. The positions of both EPA and the manufacturers would have hardened around specific emission level figures and a full-blown technical dispute likely would have erupted.

Finally, the negotiators in the wood stove regulatory negotiation shared a common desire to generate rules. Each party had their own incentives to promulgate federal rules, and each negotiator, other than those from EPA, had a strong interest in the group developing the rules rather than the agency alone. This shared goal provided the focus and impetus necessary to move the group along and away from protracted, contentious uses of technical argumentation.

Because other negotiators apparently deferred to EPA negotiators in the proceedings, an alternative interpretation of the rulemaking effort might contend that the agency was, in fact, imposing its view of scientific and technical parameters on the other participants and using this dominance to guide the development of the rules along a relatively narrow course. After all, EPA led off discussions with technical reports written by their consultants according to EPA specifications and circulated written summaries of the meetings, in effect, etching their version of discussions into the group's collective memory. More alarmingly, participants commented on EPA's refusal to consider additional evidence and arguments on certain issues. There are features of the procedure that suggest that this interpretation is not likely to be true, however.

First, while EPA may have held an advantage in regard to the initial presentation of technical information, other participants (and observers) were encouraged to present additional information or analysis. Participants, especially negotiators representing the manufacturers, the independent testing laboratories, and Oregon state, frequently did submit supplementary data and analysis on points relevant to their areas of experience and expertise and such submissions were appropriately weighed and integrated into the rulemaking.

Second, it might also be argued that the degree to which the agency tended to reject evidence counter to its own in the negotiation was no greater than its exercise of discretion in normal rulemaking. In fact, in the negotiation setting, failure by EPA to consider evidence was openly visible to participants and was thus potentially more politically costly. Participants could rebel *en masse*, if necessary, by withdrawing from the negotiation altogether. Since the parties soon organized themselves into coalitions, the displeasure of one party could result in many parties registering complaint by walking out. Thus, the damage EPA would incur by openly refusing to consider scientific evidence that contradicted their own would be substantially greater in a consensual procedure than under conventional rulemaking procedures, and the agency would be less likely to blithely overrule or neglect contrary arguments.

In any case, participants believed that their interests were better expressed and met through the negotiated rulemaking procedure in comparison to conventional proceedings. As two persons described it, "Each group got something" and "No one gave away something they really wanted."[14] Similarly, no negotiator interviewed criticized the scientific or technical soundness of the rule, although many noted gaps in information they believe might have helped to refine the rule. In fact, several participants described the resulting rules as highly creative and wise in ways that EPA would have been unable to duplicate on its own.[15]

Procedure 3: Proceeding Despite Uncertainty[16]

The mediation effort in the Michigan fishing dispute occurred as a result of a court order and came at a relatively late stage in the evolution of the dispute. Unlike the New York City case, it was unclear how prominent technical issues would become in the negotiations. Like the wood stoves case, however, key contenders in the legal battle had access to a sizable scientific and technical arsenal. Any settlement was likely to hinge critically on the perceptions of various parties with respect to major scientific assumptions.

Building Communication Linkages. The principal parties, the Michigan Department of Natural Resources (DNR), representing commercial and sports fishers, the three tribes, and the federal Department of the Interior had been engaged in legal battle for more than a decade. Relations among the parties were strained. The tribes felt the DNR only dealt with them grudgingly, treating them with increasing respect only as a result of their victories in the courts (Doherty). A series of attempts had been made over the years to negotiate a settlement to the conflict over the Great Lakes fishery, including an effort in 1982 that produced an "agreement in principle" among the key parties. But, the agreement had fallen apart when attorneys began drafting and the parties began reviewing the document (*Legal Times*).

When the special master arrived on the scene, he was greeted with a number of parties with a long history of distrust and difficult relations. He was given instructions from the court to assist the parties to reach a negotiated settlement and to manage the discovery process leading to a court trial, which was set for April 22, 1985, in the event that negotiations failed.

Special Master McGovern's strategy was built upon three elements: (1) fostering a sense of urgency to settle the dispute, (2) cultivating among the litigants a desire to have a direct hand in shaping the settlement and, (3) de-escalating the hostile use of scientific arguments. Between the months of January to March 1985, the special master met with the attorneys representing the parties on an accelerated discovery schedule. At least one attorney recalled billing his client conservatively for 250 hours per month during that period, and spending three out of four weeks obtaining depositions from witnesses for the case.

During this interval, McGovern also called a meeting inviting all interested parties, the biologists, and the attorneys, to hear remarks by participants in a similar case of litigation concerning a state-tribal fishery dispute in Washington state. The primary message at this gathering was not subtle. Many of the listeners reported that the intent was to drive home to the disputants the idea that litigation was a horrendous affair to be avoided at all costs. By convening this meeting, McGovern was apparently attempting to increase the parties' perceptions of the attractiveness of their alternative to litigation, a negotiated settlement.

Finally, McGovern brought together for several meetings biologists from the key parties (replicating almost to a person the TTWG), a nonpartisan convener, and a fish biologist with modelling expertise from the state-funded University of Michigan Institute for Fisheries Research. The stated purpose of convening the biologists was to develop a common model for predicting the impact on the fishery of varied allocation proposals.

The mediation effort culminated in an intense, three-and-a-half day negotiation set at a college in Sault St. Marie in late March 1985. More than 50 persons representing the litigants as well as interested individuals representing only themselves attended the negotiations. This sizable group was divided into two, and the smaller core, comprising representatives of the litigants, hammered out an agreement that eventually became an order of the court. At the end of a round-the-clock session that extended some 36-hours, this core group of negotiators posed for the press cameras standing behind the settlement draft that bore their signatures.

The impact of the meetings of the biologists, the special master's focussed attempt to resolve important technical issues, cannot be appraised in isolation from the other activities undertaken during the first three months of 1985 to move the parties closer to agreement. Through the discovery process, the litigants were gaining an understanding of their opponents' lines of argumentation, on both legal and technical issues having to do with the fisheries, and were culling a more refined estimate of their chances of prevailing in court. The statements from the Washington state litigants exerted subtle pressure on the parties to settle out-of-court. Nonetheless, what was achieved by McGovern's attempt to separate and zero in on the biology of the Great Lakes fisheries was both a common recognition among the litigants of the uncertainties of the biologists' assessments and recommendations, and the concurrent construction of his own evaluation of the resource, which was not particularly "expert," but which had the potential to become authoritative if the negotiators failed to reach an agreement.

An Unstable Scientific Consensus. Despite the difficulties faced by the policy makers, biologists working for the major parties had been cooperating on fishery projects for several years. The Great Lakes Fishery Commission, an international organization founded in 1956, established lake committees comprising representatives of all government agencies (in Canada and the U.S.) holding resource management responsibilities on each of the Great Lakes to study indigenous lake species and coordinate population rejuvenation efforts. In 1980, the Tripartite Technical Working Group with biologists from the Michigan DNR, U.S. Fish and Wildlife Service (U.S. Department of Interior), and the tribes' newly-formed Chippewa-Ottawa Fishery Management Authority began meeting to compile data and set annual total allowable catch (TAC) levels on certain fish species in portions of Lakes Huron, Superior, and Michigan within the boundaries of the state of Michigan. The TACs represented a published consensus on recommended levels of fish catch by zones.[17]

It would seem that the TACs published in the annual *Status of the Fishery* reports compiled by the TTWG signalled the end of any adversarial or combative uses of scientific information or advisors. The TACs determined the "size of the pie" and biologists had little to say about into whose buckets the fish should fall. In fact, however, the reports represented not a true collaborative scientific finding, but a fragile compromise that could easily shatter if placed too close to any discussion on resource allocation. The matter of who should catch the fish was only thinly disguised behind more technically drawn arguments involved in establishing TACs.

Like many so-called "technical issues," the determination of TACs requires a mix of explicitly policy decisions and less conspicuous, value-bound, professional judgments. To begin with, TAC is dependent on a prior policy decision about the desired condition of the population under consideration. If population growth (as opposed to a stable or declining population size) is desired, a rate of growth must be targeted. For example, the federal Fish and Wildlife Service placed high priority on lake trout rehabilitation. For this species, they would tend to favor policies that would foster high population growth rates, such as a low TAC level, on the presumption that lower catch levels will reduce overall mortality rates and increase the probability that the lake trout population will reproduce. On the other hand, a group less concerned about lake trout rejuvenation might favor a much higher TAC, since their concern is short-term gains associated with catching fish.

Selecting a targeted growth rate for specific fish populations is clearly a decision guided by values, interests, and policy objectives. It is only the first of a series of negotiated points the TTWG members faced along the path to determining TACs, however. The next tier of issues concerned assumptions about variables used to establish TACs given a particular growth rate target, factors such as current population size, population age structure, individual growth rates, and mortality rates. On these points, value-bound, professional judgment comes into play in a more indirect way. Although some of the factors necessary for determining TAC are less controversial than others, all are merely estimates, based on extrapolations from data from sample studies, studies of comparable populations, or multi-purpose record keeping.

The link between these assumptions and the ultimate TAC determination is quickly apparent. For example, as mentioned earlier, TAC is dependent on overall mortality rates, which are defined by two components, fish catch level and natural mortality. Fish catch levels are recorded by the Fish and Wildlife Service based on catch reports submitted by licensed fishers. The natural mortality factor is less easily ascertained, but by convention, biologists have relied on the observed mortality rates of pristine populations.

The determination of both components of fish mortality became the subject of debate among biologists whose "professional judgments" clearly reflected political values and interest considerations. The Michigan DNR staff biologists took issue with the fish catch level component in establishing the mortality rate of lake trout. While fishermen for centuries have been chided for telling "fish stories" that exaggerate their conquests, DNR policy makers conversely accused tribal fishers of seriously underreporting their incidental lake trout catches. The DNR biologists accordingly argued that the FWS figures should be inflated when determining TACs.

Increasing the catch level component of the mortality rate used to determine TACs served an obvious political purpose. In the lake trout population, the Michigan DNR argued that the incidental lake trout caught by gill nets increased overall mortality to levels that inhibited lake trout reproduction. The DNR argued that restricting gill nets would reduce lake trout mortality and foster rejuvenation, without requiring a lowering of TAC levels that would diminish recreational fishing opportunities. Since only tribal fishers use gill nets, and some tribal fishers use gill nets exclusively, this interpretation of the cause of high mortality among lake trout populations had obvious implications for the allocation contest.

The natural mortality rate was open for debate as well. In this case, the tribes' biologists argued that the proportion of overall mortality attributed to natural mortality was underestimated. They argued that the use of mortality rates of pristine populations was inappropriate to estimate natural mortality of populations in environments that have undergone significant change, such as increased chemical pollution. The political motive for this line of argumentation is also fairly obvious: tribal biologists were attempting to defend the use of gill nets by shifting some of the onus of high mortality off the incidental catch component and onto industrial society more generally.

Given the intensity of the allocation dispute, it is unlikely that the biologists were completely unaware of the distributional implications of setting high or low TACs for specific species in particular zones. Undoubtedly, even while discussing the issues in a professional manner, they were honing arguments to edge TACs upward in fishing areas favored by their respective sponsors. Nonetheless, despite such politically motivated manipulations, it seemed that as long as the issue of who is catching the fish was kept out of the discussion, the biologists were able to agree on discrete figures for the variables used to determine TACs.

Appropriating Science. Given the fragility of the apparent consensus, how did Special Master McGovern deal with the technical aspects of the dispute? The structure of this alternative dispute resolution effort differed distinctively from the previous two cases in that the "technical experts," the fishery biologists, were consciously and deliberately convened at different times and places from the attorneys or the principals. McGovern's reasoning for this was simple. First, although McGovern himself did not mention this, according to one participant, Judge Enslen believed that the biologists could talk to one another on a professional level, whereas relations among the principals were overly strained. It is likely that Judge Enslen communicated his hunch to McGovern, but whether he did or not, McGovern could easily see that the biologists had been cooperating for several years on the TTWG. He thus wanted to take advantage and not jeopardize that communication channel.

According to McGovern, he also ascertained through conversations with individual biologists that the biologists *qua* biologists were disagreeing for two reasons. First, once there was any significant uncertainty in the analysis, individuals would go off in different directions with their own estimates of the appropriate figure to assume. Secondly, and not unrelated to the first issue, the policy makers who hired them were pushing certain policies and looking to the biologists to provide supportive scientific rationales. Distancing the biologists from their employers was therefore critical in McGovern's opinion, although he could not control, of course, communications that occurred outside of these meetings.

Although the hostilities among the principals were said to have been mirrored by the biologists to some degree, McGovern hoped that he could succeed at toning down the adversarialism and political posturing by the biologists if they met without their advisees. During the series of meetings that occurred over about a three-month period, McGovern and his assisting technical facilitator, Francine Rabinowitz, an urban planning professor and member of a Los Angeles law firm, continually tried to guide the group to a consensus on technical issues based on their common commitment to the fisheries as an ecological resource and their standards of professionalism. Not insignificantly, meetings and field trips were scheduled to encourage the group to lunch, dine, and travel together. Opportunities to emphasize areas of agreement were fully exploited, as well as thoughtfully worded questions intended to "shame the biologists into recognizing their areas of agreement."[18]

McGovern attempted to deal with the first issue, disagreement among the biologists in estimating values for various variables, by encouraging the biologists from the three major parties to collaborate on building a computer-based population model of the fisheries of the Great Lakes. His strategy was to narrow the areas of disagreement on technical issues by helping the biologists to identify all the factors they could most easily agree on, insert these figures into a mutually acceptable model, and leave the variables of greatest uncertainty (and hence the most difficult to reach agreement on) for the policy makers to deal with. Ultimately, he hoped the model could be used "hands on" by the parties during negotiation to try out different allocation proposals to see who would get how much of what kind of fish in which part of the lake under differing assumptions about disputed variables. For example, negotiators would be able to compare a proposal for a straight 50 percent split of all fish stock to one based on zone assignments, or contrast two or more different zonal apportionment schemes.

The group failed to develop the model McGovern had envisioned. According to McGovern, the failure was due to two major deficiencies: a lack of resources and skepticism about models generally. His second insight was perhaps not far off the mark. At least one biologist representing a key player confided that he would never have recommended reliance on the model to his advisees because he disagreed with many of the model's assumptions.

Although the model fell short of McGovern's original expectations for it, the exercise served other important purposes. First, the exercise helped the biologists to see more clearly the points of strongest agreement and disagreement and their relative importance. For example, the degree to which gill nets increased fish mortality was a point that seemed to be beyond settlement. Suspecting the difficulty it presented and the emotional overtones of the debate, since gill nets were used exclusively by the tribal fishers, Rabinowitz encouraged the group to leave the issue unresolved. The model that was subsequently constructed was run with "high," "moderate," and "low" values for the gill net mortality variable and, surprisingly to all, the model ultimately proved insensitive to these different levels. Thus, a point that might have become a lightning rod for reopening old wounds among the biologists was adeptly circumvented.

Perhaps more importantly than creating among the biologists a common frame of reference, the collaboration of the biologists helped to develop a technical base of reference for the special master. Given the special master's privileged status before the court, the biologists would be quick to recognize the significance that the collaborative product might eventually hold. They would thus be encouraged to fight strongly for so-called technical judgments embedded in the model that have clear implications for their principals. Because the model was correlated with zones, one might suspect that biologists would fight especially hard to "win" arguments that would set technical parameters in zones important to their principals. Although the modelling effort did not bring the biologists closer to agreement on technical and scientific issues, it created an alternative "authority," that, one might argue, was a sort of composite. Consequently, the model tactically served to move the parties closer to agreement not by dissolving disagreement among the scientists, but by creating an alternative "authority" that would legitimate the special master's allocation recommendation to the court, should the parties fail to settle.

Restructuring the Use of Science

The consensus-based methods utilized in these three cases differed from one another in many respects. The degree of interaction between experts and non-experts, the duration of the consensus-based procedure, and the nature and extent of the facilitator's intervention are just three of many ways in which *techniques* differed. Nonetheless, the unifying theme for distinguishing these methods remains unmistakable. These procedures aimed to clarify, resolve, or avoid disputes on key scientific and technical aspects of a decision, while allowing political conflict to become more salient. Scientific knowledge and expertise were used to inform decisions, but without confusing debates that result from an adversarial focus on science.

As such, these methods represent substantial advances over conventional approaches toward integrating scientific information and disagreement into politically stable decisions.

Addressing Criticisms of Conventional Methods

In contrast to the methods reviewed in Chapter 2, these consensus-based methods assumed that differing scientific and technical opinions and supporting evidence can be legitimate, given the existing state of knowledge. That is, rather than to dismiss all arguments but one, or attempt to gloss over differences in scientific or technical judgments, the decision makers and stakeholders attempted to ascertain the degree of confidence that could be placed in various scientific or technical arguments. In the New York City policy dialogue, this was achieved through intense periods of questions and answers in the presence of a formidable line of individuals highly trained in relevant areas of expertise. In the wood stoves regulatory negotiation, the basis of divergent views was revealed by encouraging those with competing views to explain their interpretations or present alternative analysis. The flexible format and the longer time frame in this case allowed parties to seek and generate additional information and analysis between sessions to enrich the common knowledge base for all discussants. Importantly in these two cases, the disclosure of the basis of scientific disagreement was performed openly in the presence of contending stakeholders as well as before representatives of the decision makers. Although expert advisors hired by a particular party might share value biases that would tend to produce scientific conclusions that advantage their sponsors, the "mixed" audience format apparently operates to filter out these biases to some degree, as individuals struggle to maintain a standard of "professionalism" among their peers as well as credibility among their own clients. Thus, although stakeholders' expert advisors may concentrate on critiquing data or analysis presented by contending groups, the end result tends to be less a standoff than a joint recognition of the limits of scientific certainty.

Largely because of similar concerns about professional standards and because consensual methods appear to generate a stronger concern about clearing the air of misdirected information among all parties, scientific disagreements that were founded in illusion rather than substance were easily decloaked. "Miscommunication" tactics, such as using the same term to describe different phenomena as in the use of "worst case scenario" in the NYC case, were readily identified by stakeholders, expert advisors, decision maker representatives, or the facilitator.

The recognition of the legitimacy of contending scientific or technical arguments and the understanding that differences result from differing value judgments, force decision makers and stakeholders alike to acknowledge the inevitable intrusion of political influences into scientific disputes. Once it became clear through the policy dialogue that the CBNS risk assessments reflected, more than anything else, a far more conservative orientation toward risk, ignoring conservative attitudes could be seen as a political action. At that point, the decision makers could chose to lose political goodwill from a segment of the population or attempt to address their concerns. But, they no longer had the choice to ignore entirely the political interests behind the movement to stop the Brooklyn Navy Yard plant.

Recognizing the political nature of scientific disputes also, in a sense, appears to encourage policy players to state their concerns more explicitly. An increase in participants' understanding of competing and conflicting interests elevates the level of discussions. Groups who initially supported competing decision alternatives might discover that their interests are different, but not conflicting. In the wood stoves case, for example, the traditional rivals were the clean air advocates and the affected industry. Clean air advocates wanted a numerical standard that would result in improved air quality while the wood stove manufacturers, on the other hand, were most concerned about a compliance date that could be accommodated within existing production schedules. As long as the standard was attainable with available technology, any standard requiring modifications in stove design would require a minimum amount of time to redesign and retool production lines. Thus, although the objectives of the clean air advocates and the industry were divergent, their interests were less in conflict than appeared at first sight. Without a climate that encourages the discussion of political interests on this level, decisions that attempt to integrate such concerns are far less probable.

Finally, perhaps one of the more salient changes evident from these examples of consensus-based methods is the consistent function assigned to scientists and technical experts. Whereas the degree of discretionary decision making authority implicitly conferred onto scientists is unclear in conventional processes that place undue weight on scientific and technical factors, the role of scientists is less ambiguous when scientific and technical components are treated as guides and aids, not determinants. Consensus-based methods that are aimed at obtaining approval from all participants appear simultaneously to bring all individuals up to a common plane of technical competency. When experts are aware that they must explain the logic of their arguments rather than simply ride on their reputations to win concurrence, they too make more serious efforts to educate the stakeholders. The division between experts and non-experts narrows.

A New Role for Science

In all three cases examined, science had been, or potentially would have been, utilized strictly to support or discredit one policy alternative. Prior to the policy dialogue, the New York City dispute was a classic case of two polar opposite policy options standing head-to-head behind inconsistent risk estimates by technical experts. Although the basis for the divergences could be gleaned from a careful reading of the competing reports, the facilitated policy dialogue opened communication between reputable technical specialists and members of the concerned public, especially staff from the decision making Board of Estimate offices, and allowed an opportunity for the experts to elaborate on the reasons why ambiguities exist. In the course of their comments, they made clear that much of the cause of the uncertainty was inherent in the scientific enterprise, and was not something that could be corrected or eliminated through additional investigation or further testing, at least not within a reasonable amount of time. Thus, the discussions ended any possibility of the decision makers deferring a decision for further study or seeking authoritative guidance from scientists and it became clear that the risk assessments represented little more than varying orientations toward risk. The decision "to build" or "not to build," similarly reflected differences in a willingness to accept (or impose) a health risk.

A somewhat different dynamic prevailed in the wood stoves regulatory negotiation. Parties entered the negotiations with a fairly strong sense of the relative scarcity of pertinent scientific data and information. The "win-win" euphoria that many popular writings and workshops on negotiation exalt did not lull stakeholders into assuming that technical arguments did not matter, however. Stakeholders with access to technical studies went fully equipped and prepared to state their arguments in a manner most flattering to their interests. Nonetheless, unless their evidence was incontrovertible, the cross-examination by adversaries reduced many studies to "good guesses" rather than definitive statements. As such, the fire power of their technical support systems was dampened and stakeholders acceded to bargaining over ranges (of estimates for technical factors) and across issues.

Finally, in the Michigan fishing case, the use of science was transformed in two, interesting and distinct ways. First, debate over scientific issues concerning the biology of the Great Lakes fishery was almost entirely absent from the final negotiations. Biologists were not present in the negotiations, except as consultants to be conferred with during caucusing. Negotiating representatives of the major stakeholders simply checked back with their biologists to assess the catch implications of different allocation proposals. Apparently, the estimations of catches in different zones were not sufficiently divergent to evoke debate.

What is meant by "sufficiently divergent?" This leads to the second point. The stakeholders were negotiating under intense pressure to settle. The fishing dispute had been ongoing for years and communities were reeling under the animosity between tribal fishers and non-tribal fishers, with outbreaks of physical violence, verbal abuse, and overtly racist media commentaries. A court trial date was approaching. Each party was aware of serious defects in their legal arguments and the outcome of a trial was highly uncertain for all parties. Most importantly, the court's appointment of a special master meant that the court most likely would rule in accordance with Special Master McGovern's settlement recommendation. If the parties did not reach an agreement, a settlement would be imposed on them.

The role that science came to play in the settlement was secondary compared to what might have occurred in the courtroom. It was not used as a weapon by the stakeholders. If a weapon in any sense, it was one in hands of Special Master McGovern who through the mediation process had gained sufficient understanding of the technical issues to provide Judge Enslen with a credible technical base for an allocation decision.

If science under conventional decision making is deployed as a weapon to persuade decision makers or the polity to accept a given decision alternative, then altering the role of science through consensual approaches will have implications for the ability of different groups to exert influence over public decisions. How are the dynamics of political power affected by the use of supplementary, consensus-based methods in decisions presumed to be informed by scientific and technical information and expertise?

Notes

1. These writers contribute to what is called the "constructivist" view of science. The constructivist view looks toward the external culture that furnishes "interpretive resources" that shape scientific knowledge for political purposes. For further elaboration, see Ditta Bartels, "Commentary: It's Good Enough for Science, but Is It Good Enough for Social Action?" *Science, Technology, and Human Values*, 10(4): 69-74, 1985.

2. For a fuller discussion of these factors, see Ozawa and Susskind.

3. I will use the term "intervenor" to mean the range of roles called "convener," "facilitator," or "mediator" in the negotiation literature.

4. This phrase was used by Walter Shaub to describe the events during the policy dialogue (New York Academy of Sciences, 1984b).

5. See, for example, Commoner's *The Closing Circle*.

6. This was a reason given by Dr. Commoner during a personal interview in October 1986, at the Center for the Biology of Natural Systems, Queens College, Flushing, New York.

7. Unless otherwise noted, the following description of the Wood Burning Stoves regulatory negotiation is based on interviews listed in Appendix 1.

8. The list of participants is provided in Appendix 2.

9. See Roy J. Lewicki and Joseph A. Litterer, *Negotiation*.

10. Based on comments made by David Doniger during a telephone interview, May 1987.

11. Based on comments by R.D. Gros Jean during telephone interview, May 1987.

12. Based on comments by John Charles during telephone interview, May 1987.

13. William Becker, John Canaday, Donnis Corn, and David Doniger were among the participants who made comments along this vein during telephone interviews, May and June 1987.

14. Statements were given by David Doniger and David Swankin during interviews, May 1987.

15. Based on comments made by William Becker, John King, and Harold Garabedian during telephone interviews, May and June 1987.

16. The description of the Michigan fishing case is drawn largely from interviews conducted by the author in 1987.

17. TACs are as much policy- as science-based, because their determination is dependent on a targeted level of population growth. In other words, a mortality rate of 60 percent or 70 percent may both protect a given population, but the lower rate will be more likely to result in a higher rate of reproduction and hence population rejuvenation. Since TAC is simply the catch level correlated with given mortality rates, a TAC determination is predicated on agreement on a targeted rehabilitation rate. Biologists favoring rejuvenation over human-oriented concerns, such as short-term economic stability, for example, may support an assumption of higher rehabilitation targets and lower catch levels. Conversely, DNR biologists familiar with the state's commitment to sports fishing may tend to endorse slower (though steady) population growth rates for popular sports species, such as lake trout in tourism-dependent locales.

18. Based on telephone interview with Francine Rabinowitz, July 1987.

4

Power Dynamics in Consensual Procedures

Public decisions are often highly contentious. This is appropriate because they reallocate finite and sometimes scarce resources, and set the rules for future distributions by indicating what is valid and legitimate and what is not. For example, at stake in the Michigan fishing case was both the imminent allocation of actual fish to various groups and the more long-term allocation implicit in the recognition of the rights of each group to the fishery resource.

The responsibility for public decisions rests on the shoulders of government, namely, elected officials, administrative bodies, and the judiciary who are vested with formal decision making authority. The authority to make a decision is not the same as power in decision making, however. A decision reflects a series of prior steps such as the identification and formulation of a problem, identification of alternative solutions, and the selection of one alternative over others. A public decision is the product of conflict among competing stakeholders from the first step to the last. While official decision makers hold the responsibility and authority to determine public action, many groups contend to raise the questions before the decision makers (agenda setting), frame the issues, identify alternative resolutions, as well as to help select a particular course of action.

In this chapter, we will consider how consensual procedures can affect the mobilization of scientific and technical information and expertise in various phases of the contest over public decisions and how the distribution and dynamics of political power in decision making are changed as a result. To begin with, we look in greater detail at four phases of the decision making process. We then consider what occurred in the three cases of this study. Finally, we will attempt to draw insights about the nature of power in public decision making and how power is mediated by consensual procedures.

Mapping the Battlefield:
Science in Four Phases of Decision Making

In the section below, we will examine the use of science in four general phases of decision making: agenda-setting, problem formulation, identification of alternatives, and the decision choice. These phases do not necessarily represent distinct or sequential steps in decision making. In fact, conceptually, they sometimes overlap, and an actual decision making process may vacillate repeatedly between two or more phases. Rather, this identification of phases is intended simply to provide an analytical structure for thinking about the use of science in the evolution of a public decision. The four phases also do not exhaustively represent public decision making. Indeed, public decisions can be thought of as originating in the earliest stirrings of controversy and extending beyond the decision choice stage, since implementation and (programmatic) evaluation can change the ultimate effect of a decision on actual public resource allocations.

Science in Agenda-Setting

The first formal step in decision making is to place issues on the political "agenda." Political scientists Cobb and Elder, have described two types of political agendas. The more abstract, more general, and broader "systemic agenda" refers to a set of political controversies that are viewed as "legitimate concerns meriting the attention of the polity" (Cobb and Elder: 14). For instance, ensuring a clean and healthy environment is an issue that has gained a prominent place on the systemic agenda in the United States but has not been entered on the systemic agenda in many third world countries. As a result, in the U.S. considerable public initiative is directed toward controlling activities deemed environmentally offensive, whereas the idea of inhibiting business behavior for the sake of environmental quality in some third world countries is still regarded as subversive to a healthy economy and is, consequently, rarely taken seriously.[1]

Systemic agendas are typically the background against which more localized or specific agendas are set. Cobb and Elder refer to these as "institutional agendas," which are sets of "concrete, specific items scheduled for active and serious consideration of a particular institutional decision-making body" (Cobb and Elder: 14). A lawsuit, as in the Great Lakes fishing case, and an issue slotted for regulatory rulemaking are examples of institutional agenda items. In contrast to issues on the more general systemic agenda, items on an institutional agenda are usually tailored for a particular decision making forum and are relatively well defined. Rather than the systemic agenda item of "a clean and healthy environment," for example, a related item on the institutional agenda would be more specifically stated, such as the regulation of polycyclic organic matter, as in the EPA wood stoves case.

An issue appears on either type of public agenda when advocates for action succeed in directing sufficient public attention to the issue to pressure a response from elected officials. Two significant reasons for getting issues on the public agenda are obvious: issues that are not considered will not be directly addressed, and public resources will not be invested on issues that do not reach the public agenda.[2]

There are also more subtle consequences.

> The social and political significance of agenda-building arises in part from the fact that it serves to structure subsequent policy choices. However, the stakes involved do not reside solely in the prospects of future policies. There are more immediate payoffs involved. These take the form of social recognition and the validation of certain values, interests, and beliefs to the exclusion of others (Cobb and Elder: 171).

Agenda-setting hence not only helps to direct the future course of public actions, it also conditions the polity into accepting that certain types of actions are assigned appropriately to the public domain and to specific forums with in it.

Scientific arguments play important parts in setting both systemic and institutional agendas. In the former, they shape the emerging understanding of a public problem and in the latter they influence the way specific debates are cast. One should consider how science was used in the waste management case in attempts to place issues on both types of agendas.

We noted earlier that the New York City Department of Sanitation (DOS) successfully positioned the solid waste disposal crisis onto the institutional agenda of the Board of Estimate (BOE). The DOS issued numerous public statements about an impending crisis. Their dire predictions on diminishing disposal capacity coupled with increasing disposal needs were carefully corroborated by technical analyses performed by DOS staff. These predictions were crafted to create a sense of urgency around the city's solid waste situation in order to generate public concern and incite the BOE to act favorably. The technical analysis was location-specific, focusing on New York City, and was tailored to address that city's public governing board.

One group opposing the plans similarly used technical analysis to launch a challenge against the agency's proposal. This group focused their attack on a technical assessment of the adverse health impact of the proposed technology on the city's residents. While the immediate objective was to affect the BOE's action on the proposals, their line of argumentation also served to arouse public concern about the desirability of dioxin-emitting (or health-threatening) technology in general. In this sense, technical argumentation may be seen as attempting to bring the question of "safe" technology onto the broader, systemic agenda.

The wood stoves case presents two additional examples of the use of scientific information to strategically locate an issue on the public agenda. In this case, recall that the plaintiffs, the Natural Resources Defense Council and the state of New York, first brought forth technical evidence that suggested possible adverse health effects from polycyclic organic matter (POM) inorder to force EPA to classify POMs as a hazardous air pollutant under Section 112 of the Clean Air Act and to take correspondingly appropriate regulatory action. Then as part of the out-of-court settlement, EPA agreed to regulate one of the major emitters of POM's, wood burning stoves, which produce nearly half of total nationwide polycyclic organic matter, according to studies cited by EPA.

As these examples show, scientific arguments play an important role in placing items onto the systemic and institutional agendas. Because of the authority we as a society confer upon science and the ways that we have integrated science into our formal governing statutes (as discussed in Chapter 1), the substantiation of public concerns by scientific argument provides sufficient legitimacy to compel decision makers to act. Indeed, it is difficult today to imagine issues gaining placement on the public agenda without supportive scientific arguments.

Science and Problem Formulation

Issues that arrive on the public agenda do not develop spontaneously. Just as the placement of issues on the agenda is usually the work of groups advocating action, so is the particular form of their construction the result of conscious and deliberate efforts by stakeholding groups. From a potentially unlimited assortment of facts about a condition or situation, a specific set is selected and interpreted to identify, describe, and explain a "problem" (Wildavsky). The selection of some facts and the omission of others is usually consciously undertaken with a particular objective in mind.

The formulation of a problem can serve political purposes in several ways. First, the formulation of a problem can be undertaken with an explicit aim to generate sympathy and support from those not directly involved in policy making. The New York waste management case provides an example of the politically strategic value of problem formulation and the use of scientific argument. While residents adjacent to the Brooklyn Navy Yard site were opposed to the solid waste incinerator for a number of reasons, including a sense of being unfairly subjected to a noxious land use, their alliance with scientists from the Center for the Biology of Natural Systems presented a new way of framing the "problem." Rather than being simply a locally unwanted facility, the solid waste incinerator was transformed into a cancer-causing health threat to the entire community. Thus, instead of standing alone in their opposition to the plant, the analysis of risk posed by dioxin emissions enabled Williamsburg residents to generate support from the wider public on the basis of health and environmental concerns, in part because it was the first move in a comprehensive plan which would pose similar threats elsewhere in the city.

On the other hand, initially the DOS astutely attempted to steer clear of the health issue as much as possible. The agency's formulation of the waste management issue was built around the need for technically feasible and efficient solid waste processing, not on the need for environmentally benign technologies.

By keeping the problem focused narrowly, the DOS was also trying to assert what Gusfield has called its "ownership" of the problem. Gusfield has packaged a set of concepts under the term, ownership. He contends that ownership is attributed to or claimed by certain groups on the basis of their reputation of expertise in relevant fields. He states that,

> At any time in a historical period there is a recognition that specific public issues are the legitimate province of specific persons, roles, and offices that can command public attention, trust, and influence. They have credibility while others who attempt to capture public attention do not. Owners can make claims and assertions. . . . They possess authority in the field (Gusfield: 8).

Thus by focusing on solid waste management needs and technologies, the DOS attempted to constrain the definition of the "problem" squarely within the boundaries of its own turf (and expertise). Recast as a public health issue, the incinerator proposal would spill out beyond these lines, into areas in which the DOS held less credibility.

"Disownership" of a public policy issue, once it has been defined as a problem in a particular form, is also a strategic ploy. Gusfield cites the reluctance of the alcohol beverage industry to become involved in activities during the temperance movement as one example. Even today, he notes, the industry's slogan, "The fault is in the man, not the bottle," is a rejection of ownership of the alcohol problem. Similarly, the tobacco industry attempted to disassociate itself from the smoking problem by trying to refute the claim that tobacco smoking causes disease and instead framing the issues in terms of private choice. Gusfield also discusses two additional components of problem formulation: notions of causal responsibility and political responsibility. He writes that "causal responsibility—is a matter of belief or cognition, an assertion about the sequence that factually accounts for the existence of the problem" (p. 11). Political responsibility, by contrast, affixes an obligation for remedial action. For example, in the wood stoves case, the political responsibility for reducing particulate emissions from residential wood heating devices was set on the shoulders of government, namely EPA (as designated by Congress through the Clean Air Act). Causal responsibility was assigned to the stove manufacturers. Part of the justification for pursuing this approach to improving air quality was a belief, corroborated by technical data, that the design of many woodstoves causes higher emissions of pollutants than desired and, perhaps, than necessary. If scientific arguments could have been constructed to convince regulators and the public that emission levels are a direct consequence of wood selection (age, type, degree of wetness, etc.) and stacking rather than stove design, the regulatory approach might have been redirected to the users rather than stove manufacturers.

Finally, the formulation of problems is critical because the construction of a problem contains implications for its solution. As long as the Department of Sanitation could insist on formulating the Brooklyn Navy Yard dispute as a question of how to dispose of municipal solid wastes, they not only maintained a position of expertise but also constrained the consideration of solutions to waste processing methods, as opposed to waste reduction approaches. In the Michigan fishing case, the disputants similarly struggled to promote their own formulation of the fishery conflict. To the Department of Natural Resources, the problem was tribal fishers using large mesh gill nets in lake trout habitats popular among sports fishers. The DNR used assessment data and catch records to try to show that the tribal fishers' gill nets were causing high mortality among lake trout, which, in turn, was both retarding rejuvenation of the population and reducing the pleasure of recreational fishers. If they succeeded in portraying the dispute this way to the court, the court would have been led to consider elimination or severe restrictions on the use of gill net technology as a reasonable approach to solving at least one part of the fishery controversy.

Again, scientific argumentation is a powerful instrument in public debates because of the authority society has invested in science. Policy actors recognize that scientific evidence, selected and organized purposively, is critical for identifying and defining public problems and directs public debates from very early stages. The formulation of a problem implies who should act and in what ways.

Identifying Alternatives

As mentioned earlier, the identification of alternative solutions is largely dictated by the formulation of the "problem" (Gusfield). The way one poses a question often implies the appropriate answer, or set of answers. Posed as a "solid waste *disposal* problem," for example, the array of alternatives available to the city of New York include such actions as building a new "waste disposal" facility, extending the life of existing landfills, encouraging recycling efforts, and so on. The presumption that solid wastes are inevitable and unchangeable tends to foreclose policy actions that might focus instead on discouraging the creation of "wastes," such as regulation to limit non-reusable packaging materials, for example.

Within the bounds set by the formulation of the problem, however, usually a number of alternative actions are possible. Reflecting this, legislation and laws, such as the National Environmental Policy Act, require a consideration of alternative actions for projects proposed to meet specific objectives. Alternatives not identified, like issues not put on the public agenda, cannot be intentionally acted upon. The identification of alternatives is thus a highly political act, since it predetermines at a critical juncture what decision outcomes are possible.

In public decisions on issues that concern the environment, health, and new technologies, scientific and technical expertise is often necessary to successfully identify alternatives beyond the "no action" category. A basic concern of decision makers is that alternatives be technically feasible. For example, the technical feasibility of reducing dioxin emissions was of paramount importance in the waste incinerator case. If emissions could not be controlled, the decision alternatives would be limited to constructing the Brooklyn Navy Yard facility and accepting additional cancer risks approximated on the basis of the higher recorded emission levels from existing facilities, or abandoning the project altogether. On the other hand, if technical experts could argue (as they did) that emission reductions are possible by the installation of air pollution control technologies, potentially a range of new decision alternatives would then be identified—alternatives in technology as well as increments of cancer risk.

Hence, as is the case in an increasing number of disputes, a rather sophisticated level of technical expertise was necessary in order for participants to identify alternative actions. Technical competence, familiarity with specific technologies, and facility with scientific argumentation are, again, critical capacities for those striving to influence decision makers. Without such faculties, groups are significantly disadvantaged.

The Decision Choice

Among the array of problem formulations and corresponding alternative actions possible for each issue on the institutional agenda, the decision maker will make one choice. Although, broadly speaking, that choice is the culmination of the politics of the entire decision making process, at a certain point, the articulated choices will be limited. Then, different groups will attempt to persuade the decision maker to select alternative "A" rather than alternative "B," or "B" rather than "C."

The ways in which influence at this level is sought are multiple and complex. Often parties attempt to influence the decision maker's behavior by linking unrelated contemporary issues—i.e., political horsetrading. In the waste incinerator case, a disgruntled opponent to the Brooklyn Navy Yard project contended that certain BOE members voted to approve the project because they needed for their own reelection campaigns the endorsement of Mayor Koch, who vocally supported the proposal.[3] Similarly, one historian has suggested that the federal government's commitment to resolving the fishing dispute in the Great Lakes stemmed from President Reagan's 1980 presidential campaign promise to certain Michigan supporters to alleviate the "problem" of tribal fishers entering areas popular among sports fishers (Doherty).

Political horsetrading, though commonplace in the United States, can be a costly way to do business. In contrast, scientific arguments often make certain decision choices politically more attractive for decision makers who want to appease competing groups without trading political favors. Decision makers are strongly motivated to avoid decisions that are likely to offend a valued political constituency. Evidence that demonstrates the scientific reasonableness of a particular alternative may provide exactly the justification needed by a decision maker to defend that choice to his constituents with less risk of losing their goodwill. Likewise, policy advocates utilize scientific argumentation to persuade decision makers of the political wisdom, or at least acceptability, of opting for one alternative over another.

The wood stoves case provides a good example. Wood stoves that incorporate a catalyst device are popularly believed to burn more "cleanly," (i.e., emit fewer particulates), and more efficiently than stoves not equipped with catalysts. Given the favorable reputation of catalyst stoves, and in the absence of contrary data, EPA might have opened itself to considerable criticism had it proposed wood stove regulations that did not single out catalyst-equipped stoves as "best demonstrated technology" (BDT).

There are several political reasons why EPA might have wanted to avoid regulations that restricted BDT to catalyst stove designs, however. Foremost, manufacturers of non-catalyst designs would have been severely disadvantaged vis-a-vis catalyst stove manufacturers, and EPA probably would not have wanted regulations to seriously disrupt the industry, especially under a pro-business administration,. In addition, non-catalyst stove design manufacturers also contended that commitment to a single technology would eliminate an entire branch of innovation and would impair the development of more effective technology in the long run. Advocates of consumer rights and alternative energy technologies also were critical of a policy that would eliminate consumer choice or reduce intra-industry competition, that might eventually result in retail price increases.

Fortunately for EPA, a study in-progress reported data that appeared to confirm earlier hints that catalyst devices are often improperly used by owners, (resulting in higher emissions), and degrade through use over time. The availability of even only preliminary data was enough to discourage catalyst manufacturers, the manufacturers of catalyst-equipped wood stoves, and clean air advocates from lobbying against the "two-tracked" regulatory approach (i.e., separate standards for catalyst and non-catalyst designs) EPA ultimately proposed. Scientific data was hence instrumental in persuading EPA (and other negotiators) that a two-tracked regulatory approach was scientifically defensible and, hence, politically feasible.

Not only does scientific argumentation often play a leading role in setting the public agenda, formulating public problems, and identifying alternatives for public action, it also can provide the necessary rationale for decision makers to select one option over all others. Although it may be difficult to argue that decision makers look singularly to scientific arguments to inform their choice, the astute decision maker understands the legitimacy of decision choices that can be portrayed as consistent with technical imperatives. The savvy policy advocate recognizes the decision maker's propensity to choose such alternatives and orchestrates his own actions accordingly.

Shifting Winds of Power?

The analytic framework laid out in the preceding section highlights moments in public decision making when scientific arguments can be manipulated to influence a public decision. In the following section, we return to the three cases to examine the effect of consensus-based procedures on the role of scientific argumentation in the decision making process and the implications for these changes on the distribution and dynamics of power.

Neutralizing Science: Empowering the Underdogs

These consensus-based procedures varied considerably on many dimensions including the number and type of participants, the structure of the meetings, the goals of the meetings, and so on. The impacts of these procedures on the role of scientific argumentation in each of these cases differed correspondingly. In the first two cases, however, changes in the role of scientific argumentation appeared to affect the dynamics of power in a parallel manner. In both instances, groups initially underprivileged with respect to their ability to influence the policy decision gained power.

Consider first the facilitated policy dialogue.

The New York City dispute over the proposal to construct a municipal solid waste incinerator polarized around a technical controversy on the evaluation of the health risk posed by the facility. The facilitated policy dialogue brought together technical experts, members of the public, and representatives of the decision makers to examine critical issues pertaining to the underlying assumptions of the divergent risk assessments. After eight hours of questions and answers spoken in language relatively free of technical jargon, the audience came to understand more clearly the basis for the divergent risk assessments as well as the limits of scientific knowledge concerning the creation and destruction of cancer-causing dioxins in municipal solid waste incinerators. This clarification of the scientific disagreement altered the decision making process in two ways. First, it opened the discussion to a wider spectrum of political interests and policy alternatives and, second, it dispelled any illusion that a technical imperative for a particular decision existed.

The failure of scientists at the policy dialogue to invalidate the higher risk assessment encouraged decision makers and others to consider additional decision alternatives. One might argue that without a clear field for approving the BNY facility as proposed (which an unambiguous declaration of low risk to public health might have provided), the decision makers grew more attentive to advocates of other solid waste management methods. Although proponents of alternatives, such as recycling and source reduction, had been expressing their views publicly through the newspapers and, one may presume, privately with the decision makers, the BOE members had little incentive to listen or accommodate their interests as long as the DOS recommendations were perceived as feasible.[4] That is, why worry about small-scale waste management approaches if the massive, high-tech solution was approved? Moreover, the sophisticated technical debate held the public's attention to two simple alternatives: build or block.

When decision makers were made to feel sufficiently uncomfortable with the DOS proposal, in part as a result of the policy dialogue that affirmed the possibility of a high health risk, one could expect that the decision makers would have begun to think in terms of mitigation and ways to allay public fears of the high-tech solution. Supplementary disposal methods would reduce the tonnage of waste going into the incinerators, and the amount of dioxin coming out, and might thus newly appeal as an intermediate, compromise course.

Importantly, opening the door to additional alternatives means that supporters of these other alternatives obtained entry into the discussions and suggests that groups unable to express their political interests through an agenda framed by a highly visible technical debate gain an opportunity to be heard by the decision makers when the technical debate fades out of the foreground. That is, groups lacking sophisticated technical expertise and groups with concerns not addressed by policy alternatives directly linked to the technical debate gain a "voice." This is not to say that such groups are suddenly magically empowered to draw the attention of the decision makers. Diminishing one avenue of influence simply means that others become more prominent. Thus, whether or not groups take advantage of the opportunity depends on their abilities to exploit other channels of influence. Nonetheless, clarifying the scientific disagreement that polarizes discussions around particular decision alternatives likely creates greater receptivity of the decision makers to other viewpoints and provides an entry point that otherwise might not exist for stakeholding groups not part of the technical debate.

The facilitated policy dialogue also changed the decision making process by reducing the discretion of the decision makers to choose between alternative "A" and alternative "B." When the discussions of key scientific issues precluded a dismissal of either risk assessment as erroneous, the higher estimate developed by the CBNS team in particular could not be ignored. Decision makers who may have been inclined to go along with the city agency's recommendation, on the basis of other factors external to the issue itself, could no longer claim the mass-burn incinerator design represented safe, "proven technology." BOE members casting a vote in favor of the proposal thus became, in a sense, more accountable for their action and were forced to deal with the concerns of groups opposed to the imposition of possible, additional cancer risks on the city's residents. Once the opposing position was politically validated, (by the lack of invalidation of the supporting scientific evidence), one might presume, the political costs to the decision makers of ignoring the interests backing them increased.

The objective of the policy dialogue was simply to clarify the basis of the scientific disagreement. When the dialogue created an awareness and common acknowledgement of the level of uncertainty surrounding risk assessment and revealed the inability of scientists to completely discount either of the two, competing risk assessments, scientific argumentation could no longer be cited as a pivoting point for the policy decision. The policy dialogue thus illustrates how a consensus-based procedure can reopen a debate both to a wider number of policy alternatives and, more pointedly, to parties excluded by the technical debate. A procedure that reveals the uncertainty and ambiguity embodied in technical arguments also forces the decision maker to be more straightforward about his reasons for supporting a particular decision choice. Thus, even a simple consensus-based procedure with modest objectives regarding scientific argumentation can have a significant impact on the dynamics of power in a public decision.[5]

In contrast to the one-day facilitated policy dialogue, the wood stoves regulatory negotiation represented a rather extensive effort to generate new federal regulations. Technical aspects of multiple issues were extensively examined and debated, eventually evolving into a range of mutually acceptable approximations that then served as the basis for the rules. The institutional nature of rulemaking and the peculiar ascent of wood stove emissions onto the EPA's agenda (through the New York State/NRDC lawsuit)[6] largely defined the problem before negotiations began. But, the consensual approach to integrating scientific information and analysis into the rulemaking process seemed to enhance the abilities of stakeholding groups to influence one another and EPA, especially during latter stages. There are several ways in which this occurred.

To begin with, the structure of the consensus-based procedure simply allowed entry to many resource-poor stakeholders who ordinarily might not have gained the attention of EPA. Rather than requiring technical competence or scientific information as a ticket to effective participation in the rulemaking procedure (as is often true under conventional proceedings), the regulatory negotiation format based participation on the perception (of the agency initially and of the preliminary group of negotiators later) of which groups were likely to be most directly affected by the rules. This list of stakeholders differed distinctly from a list of those interested parties having technical competency. For example, the consumer group and a state energy office were two groups included in the regulatory negotiation that did not possess training in relevant fields of engineering, combustion physics, or environmental regulation. Under conventional notice and comment proceedings, the technical naivete reflected in the comments of these groups might have led the agency to dismiss their concerns as incongruent with factors the agency believed were technically more feasible or necessary. Through participation in the consensus-based process, as is discussed ahead, these two technically ill-prepared groups were able to put their imprint on the formulation of the emission rules and see to it that issues of direct concern to them were addressed.

Second, the regulatory negotiation enhanced the technical competency of many participants by providing an opportunity for coalitions of groups with common or non-conflicting interests to emerge and share technical expertise. A representative of a state-level environmental group stated that he depended heavily on the technical expertise of other members in a coalition of environmental and state air protection groups that he joined during the negotiation. Individuals voiced specific interests during caucusing and coalition members together discussed the implications of various technical information and developed policy proposals that were grounded in what was technically possible and sound.[7] Consequently, the interests of a group that was not independently well-equipped to handle technical aspects of the rulemaking were packaged with scientifically sound and, hence, politically persuasive arguments to an extent not otherwise likely attained.

The opportunity to form coalitions for sharing resources is especially helpful for groups that traditionally lack resources, such as public interest groups. In the wood stoves case, the "environmental coalition" relied extensively on the technical expertise of the representative from the state of Oregon and the legal and regulatory expertise of the representative from the Natural Resources Defense Council. While neither of these groups has abundant resources, together they formed a strong knowledge base from which they and other members in the coalition could benefit.

The shared sense of "mission" among members of the coalitions facilitated a sharing of technical and legal expertise. Interestingly, this same level of trust did not seem to extend beyond the coalitions into the full negotiating group. Negotiators, and technical advisors who accompanied them, volunteered relevant scientific or technical information either through writing or orally, but data and analyses were critically reviewed. Experts were subject to intense cross-examination by competent persons from contending groups during plenary sessions in which technical components of the regulatory action were discussed. This high level of skepticism within the group as a whole, however, seemed to serve constructive purposes. The process of debate appeared to educate the non-experts in the group (and elevate their status in the discussions by improving their abilities to express political interests in formats consistent with technical parameters). Such skepticism also conforms to the conventions of the scientific review process and strengthened the conviction of the group overall that their ultimate, operating consensus on "facts" was sound.

When the technical presentations and subsequent debate failed to settle the controversy to the satisfaction of the group as a whole, the issue sometimes would be tabled for further study by a smaller sub-group of the negotiators. These taskforces usually included members from the two major coalitions and the EPA, thus keeping intact the web of trust, interdependence, and credibility. At other times, according to interviewees, the EPA representatives made a unilateral judgment on the disputed technical issue.

A prejudgment by any party is seriously contrary to the spirit of a consensual approach. The fact that the other negotiators deferred to the agency suggests the real power held by EPA. One way to begin to assess the implications of this type of event is to recall that under a conventional rulemaking procedure, the agency would have the same discretion to ignore certain technical arguments. The consensus-based procedures simply failed to offer any improvement. There is another way of looking at the situation, however. In a more adversarial context, a well-publicized, persuasive technical argument could also be used to generate public pressure to force a different response from the agency. When participants quietly yield to EPA's refusal to further consider additional technical arguments in a consensus-based procedure, the agency effectively gains power. Interestingly, while several parties expressed dismay and disappointment in EPA's behavior in those specific instances, no party was sufficiently disillusioned to pull out of the negotiation process altogether. Why this was so is difficult to determine on the basis of the information gathered. The reaction of these parties may signify a number of things. It could reflect a pragmatic acceptance of the bounds of the agency's own political constraints, the fact that no group recognized personal stakes in the implications of the particular technical issues at the time, or the fact that the negotiators were truly "coopted" by the process and believed the agency's actions were proper andjust. In any case, this is an issue worth further analysis in future research.

Finally, one financially weak negotiator, the consumer group's representative, was granted funds from the regulatory negotiation resource pool to contract an economic analysis and to hire an engineering consultant. During an interview, the consumer group's negotiator said that he held the economic analysis "in his back pocket" in case he felt it necessary to present alternative arguments to EPA's economic analysis.[8] It was never shared with the rest of the negotiating group. The engineering consultant was available to all participants, but only the consumer group's representative conferred with him. Although these actions sound close to the "hired gun" approach of exploiting expertise commonly employed by policy advocates in conventional procedures, in this case, the additional capability gained by the consumer group seemed to function more as a boost to the individual negotiator's self-confidence than as an overt weapon to win "points" in the negotiations.

Generally, the regulatory negotiation presented traditionally less advantaged groups (public interest groups, groups lacking necessary expertise, groups geographically distant from the decision making locale) with considerable influence they would not otherwise have had. This case suggests that not only can destructive, polarizing effects of scientific argumentation be neutralized through consensus-based procedures, but conditions conducive to a constructive use of scientific information and analyses can be created. And, groups that lack resources and technical expertise can recover lost ground through a strategic employment of coalitions, information sharing procedures, and collaborative analysis.

In summary, both the facilitated policy dialogue and the regulatory negotiation demonstrated that consensus-based procedures can be used to broaden the spectrum of participants and enhance the ability of participants, especially those initially disadvantaged with regard to technical competency, to promote and protect their interests. Even a relatively limited endeavor such as the one-day policy dialogue can increase the opportunity of groups squeezed out of a public debate by a contentious dispute on highly technical aspects of an issue. Procedures that encourage sharing technical and scientific information and development of a common understanding of technical and scientific elements open the doors to participants who initially lack appropriate expertise. Moreover, the competency level of participants increases through debate that includes experts as well as non-expert stakeholder representatives, and all parties benefit from more comprehensive expression of concerns and fuller integration of interests into the ultimate decision choice. Importantly, stakeholders themselves may develop a sufficient understanding of technical issues to free them of their dependence on technical experts. Finally, decision makers are more accountable when technical ambiguities are resolved or straightforwardly acknowledged, and when decision makers can no longer hide behind technical arguments to justify their actions, the public overall recaptures some control of public governance.

Avoiding Minefields: Maintaining the Status Quo

The third case, the Michigan fishing dispute, provides less evidence of empowerment to traditionally less-advantaged groups. In fact, the handling of the scientific elements of the case appeared to have little impact on the power dynamics in the overall decision making process. Although the failure of the collaborative, biological modelling effort partially accounts for the relative lack of effect, it does not wholly account for it. As is discussed below, the entire negotiation mediated by the special master was directed toward unsettling the waters as little as possible.

Recall that the Michigan fishing dispute had a long history before Judge Enslen asked Special Master McGovern to help the parties involved in litigation to resolve their differences before the court hearing. Unlike the approach used in the facilitated policy dialogue and the negotiated rule-making, McGovern's strategy was to attain settlement by sidestepping the dispute's technical aspects, the controversy over the biology of the fishery, and centering discussions more on expected fish catches resulting from alternative allocation schemes than on the merits of competing models. Although parties could argue for higher catches within zones allocated predominantly for their use, in few cases were their requests challenged on the basis of perceived biological constraints. The degree of discrepancy between models was simply not significant when the allocation decisions were based primarily on dividing up large geographic zones rather than on catch levels within each zone. The handling of the scientific components of the Michigan case did not appear to affect the power dynamics among the parties in any of the ways evident in the previous two cases. It did not empower groups that were not already influential in the case by virtue of their legal standing. It also did not visibly redistribute power within the "inner circle" of negotiators. And, the procedure did little to further the stakeholders' (or anyone else's) understanding of the fishery.

The major attempt McGovern made to deal with disagreement over biological aspects of the fishery was the collaborative modelling effort, described in Chapter 3. The special master had hoped that by convening the biologists separately from the stakeholders and their legal representatives, he could resolve disagreements over biological aspects of the fishery and move the stakeholders away from bickering over scientific issues to concentrate more fully on the distributional conflict. Indeed, a common model predicting fish populations in various zones of the lake, if constructed in a consensual manner, might have been a powerful asset for bargaining over "who gets what." Unfortunately, the model proved to be both overly complex and controversial. Despite the efforts of the facilitators,[9] the biologists did not reach sufficient agreement on critical factors, and the resulting model had neither the technical capacity nore the political credibility to operate as McGovern had initially intended. The biologists returned to their respective advisees with little change in their understanding of the lakes' fishery and the parties continued throughout the negotiations to work from different models of the fishery, as provided by their partisan biologists.

As structured, even if it had been successful, the collaborative modelling effort failed to extend entry into decision making to groups beyond the major litigating parties. Only biologists from the Michigan Department of Natural Resources, the U.S. Fish and Wildlife Service, and the tribes' Chippewa-Ottawa Fishery Management Authority were invited to attend the sessions. Notably absent at the meetings were representatives from the sports fishers' or the commercial fishers' organizations.

The sports fishers believed, apparently correctly, the the state shared their interest in maintaining a healthy recreational fishery. Lack of participation in the technical discussions was not perceived by them to threaten their welfare, and, in fact, their interests were fully protected by the NDR during the negotiations.

In contrast, the commercial fishers did not fare as well. Indeed, if any one group ended up with the short straw in the deal, it was the commercial fishers. An attorney for the commercial fishers' organization expressed doubt that scientific or technical arguments on behalf of this clients would have had any positive impact, however.[10] Moreover, he stated that, had he been asked, he would have advised his clients to save their money rather than to finance an expert consultant or studies to support their claims. He believed the combined political strength of the federal government and the state of Michigan were too overpowering for the commercial fishers to successfully challenge, even with solid technical arguments. It's difficult at this point to be certain whether this attorney's statements were based more on hindsight than on his thoughts at the time. However, if these statements did accurately reflect his thinking, it is unlikely that the commercial fishers would have joined the technical collaboration even if invited, at least not without financial assistance.

Management of the technical issues also appeared to have little effect on the relative abilities of members of the "inner circle" of negotiators to influence the settlement. Consider, for example, the three Native American Indian tribes who had joined forces in the litigation despite their different interests and priorities. The special master seemed to accept the union of the three tribes without questioning their relationships to one another, perhaps at the expense of the agreement's durability, as indicated by the stated and implied imperfections of the settlement.

Of the three tribes, the numerically largest tribe, the Sault St. Marie tribe, appears to have been the most satisfied with the agreement. The members of the Bay Mills tribe were sufficiently dissatisfied with the agreement to instruct their attorney to file a suit against the negotiated agreement, which he did, and lost. And, according to the attorney for the Grand Traverse Band, the southernmost tribe felt that their interests were sacrificed by the two tribes to the north. Their attorney also said that he believed the biologist who ostensibly represented all three tribes as the head biologist of the joint Chippewa-Ottawa Fishery Management Council, was actually preferentially loyal to the Sault St. Marie tribe.[11] If true, the "lumping" of the three tribes' representation on the scientific issues may have been a critical oversight from the perspective of the two, numerically smaller tribes and the outside intervenor called in to facilitate a lasting agreement. Without access to alternative expertise, and without even the opportunity to hear the tribes' biologist in action amongst biologists from the rival groups, such suspicions could be neither confirmed nor laid to rest.

Finally, it is unclear that either the collaborative modelling attempt or any less ambitious methods employed during the negotiation measurably improved the stakeholders' understanding of the fishery. They essentially continued to believe in the partisan representation projected by their paid biologists.

Given the relative ineffectiveness of attempts to generate a common understanding of the fishery, it is difficult to conclude the the methods applied by McGovern to deal with biological issues altered the distribution and dynamics of power in the overall decision making process. However, the negotiations may have significant consequences for the dynamics and distribution of power in future exchanges among the three major parties. One reason that the negotiations succeeded in achieving an agreement was because the pie was enlarged, so to speak. Issues concerning fish planting locations, fishing gear technology, technical assistance, and hard cash were added to the original allocation dispute. As a result, in addition to the quantity of fish allocated implicitly though the assignment of fishing rights in certain zones, the tribes gained exclusive rights to fish in other areas, technical assistance, and more that $1.5 million dollars from the federal government and the state of Michigan for use toward improving their fishery management and developing an implementing an economic development program (*United States v. Michigan*). Enhanced fishery management capabilities will certainly strengthen the tribes' ability to marshall technical data supporting their political claims in future skirmishes over the fishery, which will undoubtedly arise during the 15-year life of the agreement, and in the renegotiation of the agreement scheduled for the year 2000.

Consequences for Power

As argued earlier, the ability to influence public decisions often correlates strongly with the ability to wield scientific arguments. The examples in the last section suggest that consensus-based procedures, by intent or otherwise, alter the manner in which scientific information and expertise is folded into decision making and can reconfigure the designs of influence in every phase of the process. Moreover, the three cases in this study also show that such procedures produce effects that alter the role of scientific argumentation and technical expertise in different ways, depending on the particular methods employed, and the effects on the distribution and dynamics of power vary accordingly.

Consensus-based procedures can enhance the abilities of less resource-rich groups to influence public decisions in each phase of the decision making process described earlier. Although the agenda is usually formed before a consensus-based procedure is introduced, the outcome of such procedures can essentially reset it. One might argue that through consensual devices such as information sharing and collaborative analysis, stakeholding parties initially acting in response to proposals raised by another party gain knowledge and insights that lead them to expand the agenda, raising new issues that are linked to but distinct from the original one(s). For example, although the main agenda item of the regulatory negotiation (emission standards for wood stoves) was fixed by the Environmental Protection Agency, minor issues (such as a user's manual) were added by negotiation participants as they developed a deeper understanding of the scientific basis and technical and political constraints of regulatory options, and were consequently better able to understand and articulate their interests. Groups other than the regulatory agency or ones without sufficient resources to litigate were hence enabled to add items to the agenda.

Consensus-based methods, such as information sharing and collaborative analysis, can similarly enable resource-poor groups to reformulate the policy problem under consideration as such groups become more aware of their interests and more effective at protecting and promoting them. The policy dialogue, which did not involve the sharing of new information as much as the simple clarification of information already public, enabled groups not actively engaged in the dominant technical dispute to revise the way in which the policy question was conceived, raising questions about public safety and definitions of municipal wastes along with queries about waste disposal technologies.

Knowledge of technical and political parameters of policy questions also can be critical for generating feasible options for public action. Consensus-based procedures that incorporate efforts to identify and openly discuss such parameters provide participating stakeholders with a substantial advantage for developing policy alternatives that are acceptable to the decision makers but also meet their own concerns. The wood stoves regulatory negotiation provided all participants with a richer understanding of both technical and political components of regulatory actions and enhanced the ability of all to formulate regulatory alternatives that met technical as well as political constraints and objectives.

The facilitated policy dialogue helped to broaden the list of alternatives by clarifying the basis for the discrepant health risk estimates and confirming that neither of the alternative assessments was invalid. When the scientific controversy cooled somewhat, debate could be refocused on additional alternatives beyond the two linked to the disputed risk assessments. Importantly, groups articulating policy options not directly related to the risk estimates gained an opportunity to speak and be heard, since the decision makers were less preoccupied by the technical controversy. A less contentious use of science in public decision making can strengthen the voices and concerns of groups that lack technical expertise or the financial resources to acquire it. In effect, consensus-based procedures widen participation in a very meaningful way.

Finally, consensus-based procedures can strengthen the ability of parties to influence the decision maker's decision choice. In the New York City case, advocates of recycling, waste source reduction, and other waste management alternatives gained ground when incinerator proponents were unable to invalidate the higher health risk estimates at the policy dialogue. The outcome of the policy dialogue make it politically costly for the Board of Estimate members to approve the incinerator proposal without reservations and at considerable political expense. Participants in the regulatory negotiation essentially delivered the decision choice to the official decision making body, the EPA, by producing rules consistent not only with the interests of participating stakeholders but also with what was understood about the science of wood combustion and stove technology. To ignore the recommendations of the negotiating group would have cost EPA a tremendous loss of public credibility.

In contrast, the Michigan fishing dispute case shows that consensus-based procedures vary considerably in their handling of scientific components and that the benefit to stakeholding groups is not always clear nor awarded equitably or in any consistent pattern. Disagreements over data and the biology of the Great Lakes' fishery were not resolved during the negotiations. Instead, the technical issues were simply submerged by a concentrated effort on the part of the special master to keep attention focused away from controversial, biology-based rationales for fish allocations. This approach did not appear to preferentially benefit any of the stakeholding groups nor to noticeably alter the dynamics of power among the primary negotiators.

Understanding Power

Consensus-based procedures can be structured to create disincentives for adversarial uses of scientific argumentation and to encourage cooperation and collaboration that can lead to an increased understanding of scientific and technical elements for all participants. Such an enlightened attitude toward scientific information is disruptive to power (im)balances that are based on the ability to wield scientific arguments, which is often the case in conventional decision making, because groups that typically lack the resources necessary to effectively exploit scientific and technical arguments gain access to technical information, access to expertise and, what we may call, voice and standing. These three items are critical elements of power in public decision making, especially when scientific argumentation is exploitable. Consider each of these more closely.

Access to Technical Information. We are said to be living in an "information society." Whereas in earlier eras, finance capital or control of machine technology were considered the major critical elements of power, today control over or access to valuable information is also vital to establishing political economic prominence. In public decision making, from the simple awareness of the imminence of a decision to knowledge of the most minute details regarding a given technology, information strengthens one's ability to discern and articulate specific interests and concerns. In decisions that involve technology or environmental impacts, technical information is crucial.

Technical information, however, is typically not equally available to all stakeholding groups. Financially well-endowed groups, highly organized groups, and groups proposing specific, controversial actions often have unique access to technical data and analysis. Industry, for example, by virtue of its proprietary interests in developing a given technology (such as wood stoves) often has substantial data compiled through years of product development. Many large companies also keep health records of employees and understand long before public health professionals the adverse impacts of particular substances on the human body, as we have learned from the history of the asbestos industry in the United States. Financially well-endowed groups can easily commission necessary data collection and analysis. Highly organized groups can readily mobilize members for information gathering and polling activities. In contrast, *ad hoc* groups frequently lack both organization and financial resources, and encounter substantial difficulty in locating technical information in forms pertinent to their concerns.

The sharing of information is a necessary component of consensus-based methods that include collaborative problem-solving, since all participants must work from a common understanding of the factual basis of a given situation in order to develop mutually acceptable options for resolution. Thus, groups with a private reservoir of data are more likely to bring forth this information in order to maximize the possibility for reaching an agreement. Moreover, since credibility is critical in consensus-based procedures, participants might be hesitant to withhold information, fearing adverse consequences of such bad faith behavior, namely the loss of effectiveness within the negotiating group or even dissolution of the process altogether.

The structure of these incentives does not mean that participants "take turns" in submitting information. Those holding more information may easily share more and even a greater proportion of the total information that they hold. These incentives also do not mean that participants will "tell all." It is naive to expect that the sharing of information will not be a calculated activity. However, a consensus-based procedure constructed to encourage information sharing is likely to result in greater disclosure of information than adversarial procedures and hence lead to increased access for all participants.

Access to Expertise. Information access alone is an insufficient basis for launching an effective campaign to influence a particular decision. Equally important is the wherewithal to utilize the information. In the highly legalistic framework of government activity, legal expertise is invaluable in interpreting the significance of various regulatory notices. Similarly, in cases involving the impact of technology on sensitive ecosystems or human health, specialized technical expertise is critical in order to craft credible arguments pertaining to technological feasibility or scientific soundness in defense of favored decision options.

Again, financially well-endowed groups initially hold a significant edge over less well-endowed groups. Such groups would not only be more likely to hire appropriate expertise, they would also be more likely to support an organization to coordinate the input from experts. In contrast, less-endowed *ad hoc* groups, such as neighborhood action committees or environmental coalitions, may need to rely on volunteer consultations from civic-minded researchers, and may experience difficulty in sorting through and integrating advice from different specialties.

Consensus-based procedures can be designed to extend access to pertinent expertise in a number of ways. Joint sessions with technical specialists and non-technical stakeholder representatives enable groups unable to bankroll their own technical consultants to question specialists in person. To the extent that specialists are encouraged to avoid jargon and to be responsive to questioning, all participants will have the opportunity to acquire a clearer understanding of pertinent technical information and the technical constraints of decisions. A structure that allows the formation of coalitions also enables parties to pool their resources with respect to expertise. Finally, resources allocated to the decision making process can be appropriated to hire experts selected by the participants to reduce perceptions of partiality on the part of technical advisors.

Voice and Standing. Finally, a party in a science-intensive dispute is severely disadvantaged unless it has voice and standing. "Voice" is the ability to express concerns and interests in language that is comprehensible and credible to the decision makers. "Standing" is the necessary legitimacy, conferred either explicitly through statutory language identifying those groups holding legal recognition as affected parties, or less formally, through public consensus earned by generating widespread popular support.

Both increasing access to information and expertise can enhance the ability of resource-poor groups to state their concerns in ways that appear congruent with technical parameters and, hence, improve the ability to speak more persuasively to decision makers and others. By gaining knowledge and competency in technical aspects of decisions, groups can improve their voice and standing.

Often, *ad hoc* community groups lack a voice in public decision making because their concerns, while real, are not expressed in terms that are relevant to the decision makers. There are at least two reasons why this is so. First, the group's concerns may simply not be included on a decision maker's list of decision criteria. For example, while a resort development proposal may be evaluated with regard to its impact on the physical environment and local and regional economies, the effect of an influx of profligate and well-clad vacationers on the psyche of the local adolescent population is often beyond the scope of concerns recognized in evaluative documents such as the environmental impact statement. Decision makers look to such documents to frame the issues they consider in their decision. Thus, even though a community representative may attempt to bring such issues to the attention of the decision makers, their comments may pass virtually unheard.

Second, when decision makers are bound by statutes to ensure that their decisions are technically feasible and scientifically sound, they may tend, consciously or not, to listen more attentively to concerns and resolutions that are expressed in correspondingly appropriate technical language or backed by prestigious credentials. Not only will one speaking Greek not be understood, one speaking plain English may be effectively unheard when the listeners are tuned in only to policy options rationalized with specialized terminology.

The underlying presumption in this discussion is that scientific information, knowledge, and expertise are important sources of power in decision making by virtue of the authority popularly awarded to science. They are used to identify and define a problem and its solutions, and to persuade potential political allies and decision makers to support and choose among alternative actions.

The three cases studied here suggest different ways in which consensus-based procedures can affect the dynamics and redistribute power among the players in science-intensive public decision making. The degree and type of "power" that was affected ranged from the opportunity to speak, to a shared grip on scientific information and technical tools. The effects varied according to the particular methods employed in the procedures and, hence, no clear and consistent paterns in the use of science and its implications for decision making power emerged except that a consensual approach did not permit the monopoly of scientific information and analysis by one group.

It is commonly feared that when science is deemphasized in discussions, brute force and political arm twisting by the more powerful actors take over and control decision making. This analysis of consensus-based procedures suggests contrary conclusions. Instead, by neutralizing the advantages awarded those with the financial resources able to purchase scientific information and expertise, consensus-based procedures may allow for more democratic decision making. Groups excluded from discussions because of their inability to utilize scientific argumentation gained entry into the process. Groups less fluent in relevant specialized languages gained competency and strengthened their voice.

At the same time, what resource-rich groups gave up with respect to their edge on technical matters, they may have recouped by learning more about the reservations and objections of the opposition, by helping to shape a decision that will be durable and implementable, as well as by gaining other benefits. Of course, the ability to exert real influence is contingent not only on the command of these three elements. It is also determined by an actor's relative qualities as measured against those of competing parties. That is, my ability to influence your decision regarding the purchase of a new car probably depends as much on my ability to muster up a persuasive argument as on the absence or presence of competing views. Similarly, the effectiveness of pro-life activists in influencing national abortion policy is tempered by the strength of the pro-choice movement and how well such views are articulated.

In the next and final chapter, we consider the advantages and disadvantages of consensus-based procedures for stakeholding groups, scientists or experts, and decision makers. After all, despite potential benefits of consensus-based procedures with respect to the role of scientific information and argumentation, decision making occurs in a wider context involving many other factors. The overall desirability and wisdom of engaging in a consensus-based procedure must be evaluated with respect to both the benefits and the costs of these other considerations.

Notes

1. Although, increasingly, governments of third world countries are attempting to link environmental quality with economic aid in discussions with international lending institutions and development agencies, as in the "debt-for-nature swap" discussions.

2. Note that an active policy actor may also successfully promote its interests by *preventing* the listing of an issue onto the public agenda. See Peter Bachrach and Morton S. Baratz (1962) "Two Faces of Power" *American Political Science Journal*. 56(4): 947–952.

3. Based on a personal interview with Barry Commoner at the Center for the Biology of Natural Systems, Flushing, New York in October 1986.

4. In an 80-page report, the Environmental Defense Fund claimed New York City could recycle 40 percent of its solid wastes by 1992 at far lower economic cost than incinerators (*New York Times*, August 4, 1985).

5. The proposal for the BNY facility that was approved by the BOE in the summer of 1985 included stricter monitoring provisions (to avert human and mechanical failures) and was coupled with a commitment by the DOS to more vigorously pursue recycling as a method of reducing municipal solid waste. The extent to which the policy dialogue itself contributed to this change can not be determined, but the decision choice evidently was broadened beyond the prior "build or block" framework. Interestingly, the state of New York issued a report in 1987 that recommends steps to reduce municipal solid wastes by 50 percent over the next decade (*New York Times*, January 7, 1987). The report also recommends continued reliance on incinerators.

Despite the modifications to the BNY proposal, opposition to the plant continued, which suggests the still incomplete accommodation of conflicting political interests. State hearings for necessary permits were delayed more than a year by a lawsuit. Incineration became a major issue in the 1989 mayoral election of Mayor David N. Dinkins, who called for a moratorium on incinerator development. In November 1989, New York State's environmental commissioner denied the project a necessary permit pending submission of an adequate ash disposal plan (*New York Times*, November 16, 1989).

6. Their out-of-court agreement stipulated that EPA would address PM10 and POM emissions through regulating wood stoves under New Source Performance Standards of the Clean Air Act.

7. Telephone interview with John Charles, Oregon Environmental Council, May 1987.

8. Personal interview with David Swankin, Consumer Federation of America, May 1987.

9. Special Master McGovern was assisted by Francine Rabinowitz in the facilitation of the modelling effort. Rabinowitz is a professor in urban planning at UCLA and has extensive experience with statistical modelling. A biologist from the state of Michigan-funded Institute of Fisheries at the University of Michigan provided "nonpartisan" expertise, particularly in fishery modelling.

10. Conveyed in a telephone interview with Nino Green, August 1987.

11. Telephone interview with William Rastetter, August 1987.

5

Prospects for Change

Miscast Roles for Science in Public Decision Making

From putting a man on the moon, to beginning human life in a test tube, to the ultimate feat of rendering the planet uninhabitable to most life forms, the tremendous potential for human development made possible by the accumulation of scientific knowledge is staggering. Whether one agrees or disagrees with the uses to which this knowledge has been applied, knowledge gained through "the scientific method" has tangible, material results. It is unquestionable that the body of scientific knowledge and the methods by which it has been obtained can make a substantial contribution toward understanding our world and the alternative futures before us. Few of us would welcome public (and private) decision making that completely ignores the advice of those with scientific expertise and knowledge.

As argued in Chapter 1, however, scientific information and argumentation have multiple and diverse uses. Lawmakers and other architects of public decision making procedures include scientific rationales in decision making criteria ostensibly as a means of ensuring the political accountability of decision makers. Requirements for "rational" proposals are intended to counterbalance more overtly political pressures in decision making. During the latter years of the first half of the 20th century, a period of U.S. history in which the scientific community appeared to offer an alternative perspective to the self-interested preferences of private industry, who were believed to be manipulating "captured"[1] agencies, such an approach seemed appropriate.

We have since found that disciplinary and other breakdowns of scientific knowledge can render more than one interpretation of reality, however. A question can be answered in several ways, each equally "valid" from a scientific viewpoint, the differences reflecting our incomplete understanding of objective reality and the values-bound nature of scientific methodology itself. Scientific methodology is an organized approach for gathering information that is dependent on theory, which guide the recognition, ordering, and interpretation of events, and the development and selection of theory is highly susceptible to the forces of political ideology. Hence, differences in scientific opinion often simply mirrors political competition.

Divergent scientific conclusions and predictions about the physical world enable groups and decision makers advocating competing policy alternatives to each cite supportive scientific arguments. As a result, symbolic uses of science, i.e., to legitimate decisions and decision alternatives in order to generate political support and acquiescence, have become dominant functions of scientific advising in public decision making.

Debate on scientific aspects of a decision also diverts attention from underlying political conflicts and skews public discourse in a technical direction. Because the relative ability of different stakeholding groups and decision makers to take advantage of scientific arguments is unequal, a focus on scientific aspects serves to advantage groups with greater access to the scientific establishment. Contenders on one side may attempt to center attention on scientific aspects of an issue to limit participation and the issue agenda under discussion.

Scientific knowledge has been inappropriately identified as a tool for ending dissent. As the New York City case demonstrated, resolving scientific disputes does not resolve political conflict. Settling the disagreement over risk levels by clarifying the basis of the uncertainty did not end the dispute over the mass-burn incinerator because it is political interest, not scientific disagreement, per se that fuels opposition in the first place. Whatever the risk from dioxin emissions, the Williamsburg community, for example, is one group that would likely continue to oppose the incinerator for a number of socially credible reasons, ranging from the undesirability of an incinerator in the neighborhood, to concerns about the city's lack of respectfulness toward the community. The neighborhood's political interests conceivably could have included protecting the health of residents, preserving real estate values, and concern about participation in city policies directly affecting residents. Even if the DOS could have shown that the proposed incinerator posed no increase in cancer risk, Williamsburg inhabitants likely would have continued to perceive great losses to their quality of life.

The tentative nature of scientific knowledge prevents possibilities for insuring accountability or ending controversy in public decision making. False hopes have been propagated regarding the role of scientific knowledge. The resulting contentious uses of science by groups striving to dominate public decision making have imposed serious, even if not easily quantified, costs on society, including long, protracted disputes, reversals of decisions, and inconsistent policies. Instead of decisions that synthesize political contests and scientific knowledge, the politics of decision making are obscured, stakeholders are excluded from participation, and decision makers are required to act without a reasonably sound understanding of pertinent scientific information.

Recasting Science Through Consensus-Based Procedures

Science is not limited to the roles in public decision making described in Chapter 1. Scientific information can inform stakeholders and decision makers of the feasibility and desirability of decision alternatives without being used explicitly as a tool to persuade others. It can be used to mark the bounds for discussions of political interests, but boundaries delineated through a process that accommodates divergent scientific viewpoints are a less imposing means of controlling discourse than are those set by the arbitrary adoption of a singular scientific interpretation.

With less imposition of science, a narrowly framed technical debate can otherwise be opened to a discussion of political interests. Participation need not be restricted by expertise. Decision making participants can devote their attention to a consideration and resolution of conflicting, competing, and compatible political interests rather than struggling to legitimize one representation of the technical premises over others. Resources can be directed more pointedly toward addressing the political competition and conflict that motivate controversy, and stakeholders and decision makers alike can gain a richer understanding of the issues and interests involved. And, stakeholders and decision makers can recapture the subtle unauthorized, decision making power technical experts wield through their mastery of technical argumentation.

The three case studies illustrate three different, consensus-based procedures that reformed the integration of scientific work into the decision making process. Table 5.1 summarizes the objectives, structure, primary techniques, degree of consensus, transformation of the role of science, and the impact on decision making of each consensus-based procedure argued in the previous chapters. In all cases, science was transformed from a potentially destructive weapon into a more benign tool to guide a decision making process based on political considerations.

The wood stoves rulemaking case is one example of a more constructive use of scientific knowledge. The negotiating group spent a considerable amount of time and resources on developing the technical basis of the rule. While participants undoubtedly submitted arguments they hoped would reinforce preferred policy decisions, the overriding, collective objective of the technical discussions was to establish a reasonable estimate of the technical parameters of the problem. The explicit understanding among the group—that details of the regulations would not be finalized until the rule was considered in its entirety—enabled the parties to give up obstinate battling on technical points that were unresolvable within the existing time frame for developing regulations. The group was able to operate in this manner because they shared an acceptance of the uncertain nature of air quality regulation (in terms of both the physics of wood stove combustion

Table 5.1 Distinctive Features of Three Consensus-Based Procedures

	PROCEDURE 1
Objective	Understanding the basis of scientific agreement
Mechanics of Process	Single all-day negotiating session Stakeholder representatives, technical experts, and decision maker representatives meet together No press invited, no press coverage
Techniques	Presentation by technical experts Question and answer period Facilitator attending to communications
Degree of Consensus on Technical Issues	Understanding effect of different value judgments on technical analysis Clarification of relationship between technical judgments and policy prescriptions
Transformation of Role of Science	Tool to generate public support into Expression of different orientations toward risk
Impact on Decision Making	Forces decision makers to be more accountable for actions Opens up debate to additional issues (decision alternatives) Opens participation to groups lacking technical capabilities

PROCEDURE 2	PROCEDURE 3
Building a technical consensus	Proceeding despite uncertainty
Multiple 2-3 day meetings over a 6-month period Stakeholders, experts, and decision makers meet together Deadline imposed by regulatory protocol Minimal press coverage	One multiple-day negotiating session Separation of scientific experts and stakeholder representatives Deadline fixed by trial court Orchestrated press coverage
Presentation by technical experts Question and answer period Facilitator attending to communications Additional data gathering and analysis Intervals between technical presentations and discussions to allow for further consultation and evaluation	Data sharing among technical experts Collaborative model-building (attempted) Costs of non-settlement stressed by third-party intervenor
Agreement on uncertain nature of scientific analysis and regulatory actions Agreement on ranges of plausible estimates of technical factors	Tactical accord on scientific factors Agreement to continue research on disputed scientific factors
Decision maker's rationale or basis of stakeholder's challenge into Information to define limits of possible decision alternatives	Instrument to persuade judge into Information to reassure each party that conditions of settlement minimally meet needs
Resource-poor groups gain ability to promote political interests Participating stakeholders gain influence over decision maker	Stakeholders gain better understanding of competing party's interests Diminishes appeal of reverting to conventional decision making

and the effect of regulatory controls) and a mutual respect for each group's political stake in the regulations.

In the Michigan fishing case, far less consensus on technical aspects of the dispute was attained. Agreement on a comprehensive picture of the fishery, (the number of fish in a specific zone of the lake, the impact of large mesh gill nets, and so on), was shown to be unnecessary in order for the parties to reach an accord on dividing up the fishery resource. Instead, scientific knowledge was utilized by each party to reassure it that the conditions specified in the negotiated decision were sufficient to enable it to satisfy its own objectives. There were effectively three different maps of the existing fishery and three different visions of its future evolution. The negotiating group spent less time trying to persuade one another of the "correctness" of their biological model of the fishery or the technical merits of their positions, and concentrated instead on simply procuring an agreement that met their party's needs and desires. Such an approach to using scientific knowledge and expertise is consistent with a conceptualization of scientific work as a politics-bound method for defining and understanding reality.

As these cases demonstrate, scientific argumentation can be partially set aside and technical disputes need not be resolved before politically acceptable decisions can be made. An urgency to arrive at a decision and a common goal of full participation in the decision making process are factors that can encourage stakeholders to cooperate and focus on dealing with political differences, rather than continuing on a purely adversarial and destructively competitive mode.

Of the three cases, the facilitated policy dialogue on the proposed mass-burn incinerator was designed most purposely to establish a consensus on a comprehensive view of scientific issues relevant to the proposal. In a sense, the NYAS sponsors were attempting to develop one vision of reality. The consensus that was intended, however, was not one of rallying behind one risk assessment over another, but simply one acknowledging variations in risk assessment, that, scientifically, are equally plausible in the face of incomplete knowledge.

The facilitated policy dialogue clarified not only scientific aspects of the proposal, but also the sensitivity of scientific interpretations to political interests. Asking the question, "How do discrepant assessments arise?" begs the question, "Why do discrepant assessments arise?" By confirming the legitimacy of a range of risk assessments, the process indirectly also elevated the status of corresponding political interests. In the New York case, the higher risk assessments reflected a more conservative approach to accepting (and imposing) risk. In effect, a consensual procedure can open the door for a discussion of political interests.

Variability in technical analysis is used by groups to strengthen their case against a particular policy alternative or decision. However, the level of political conflict is not only a function of the variability in technical analysis. On the contrary, political differences are the source of the passion for technical disputes. If the variation in risk assessments by the CBNS researchers and the Hart team had been 24-fold and not 240-fold, it is likely that the dispute would not have escalated on the technical front, but the Williamsburg community, as previously argued, undoubtedly would have continued their vehement opposition to the Brooklyn Navy Yard project site.

Thus, while these cases show that politically acceptable decisions can be made without resolving disagreements on scientific or technical points, resolving disagreements on scientific elements will not settle political conflict.

Importantly, subordinating scientific aspects to political concerns in policy debates through the use of consensual procedures does not mean that the value of scientific knowledge is belittled. If any group assesses the implications of a decision alternative as seriously adverse, that group always has the option of vetoing the choice. If their objections are ignored by others, they can withdraw from the process entirely. A consensus-based procedure cannot advance with unbridgeable dissent. Thus, in a sense, consensual procedures accommodate a full range of alternative interpretations of reality and the future. The consensual nature of decision making also will prevent decisions that have a chance of resulting in consequences to which any one group objects. Accordingly, decisions may tend to be conservative from a scientific perspective, since even the more extreme scientific interpretations will be given consideration.

Procedures that give prominence to political disagreement are likely to give rise to objections by those concerned about opportunism on the part of participants. That is, how can we be sure that consensual procedures will not produce decisions that satisfy political demands at the expense of scientific soundness? As long as scientists and persons with relevant technical expertise are included in the consensual procedure, their advice is unlikely to pass unheeded since, if it does, they may make their dissent known to the wider public, which will diminish the public crediblity of the negotiated agreement, threatening its viability and the usefulness of the entire exercise. In light of this, even if non-technically trained stakeholder representatives favor a particular decision alternative on the basis of political criteria, strong dissent by experts on technical grounds will likely prevent its acceptance.

Moreover, a consensual procedure potentially offers greater insurance against scientifically unwise decisions than conventional, adversarial processes. In a consensual procedure, participating scientists have more incentive to work together as colleagues in a common quest for knowledge. The consequent peer pressure to behave in accordance with the norms of the scientific community rather than in response to external pressures, (such as pressure from financial sponsors), can serve to embolden individual scientists to speak out even if doing so might invalidate a technical argument that supports their sponsor's preferred policy alternative. In effect, a consensus-based procedure can offer protection to "whistle blowers" and enhance the integrity of the technical basis of decisions.

Viability of Consensus-Based Procedures

Indeed, the cases studied in this inquiry suggest that consensus-based methods of decision making can offer opportunities for a more thorough and less contentious, though not less skeptical, review of scientific and technical components of a decision. Clearly, however, certain groups may perceive a loss of decision making influence and power. If industry has the upper hand with regard to access to data, analysis, and expertise, why would industry agree to participate in a process in which they may lose some of their advantage? If government bodies have the authority to make decisions with only perfunctory requirements for public consultation, why would agencies and elected decision makers wish to complicate matters by involving other parties? If environmental advocacy groups make national headlines when they file a legal suit against a federal agency, why would they want to quietly expend their precious time and resources on relatively colorless negotiations? If scientists have a direct line to the decision maker, why would they want to join a process in which their voice becomes only one among many?

Each group clearly has something to lose by negotiating with competitors and agreeing to accept anything less than 100 percent of their demands. Consensual approaches generally present a certain loss of control over decision making for all parties. The still largely *ad hoc* nature of the design and application of these methods means that each experience is unique and, to a significant degree, unpredictable. The peculiar mix of issues, interests, and individual negotiators may give rise to unexpected alliances and even reshape the agenda. Coalitions can form and shift the balance of resources. Factors such as negotiator personalities and rapport among negotiators, the intervenor's style and range of services, and so on, exert differing pressures on individual negotiators that are still not well understood and not easily predicted. Facilitation techniques achieve intended objectives sometimes and fail at others. In short, decision making that is redirected by a consensus-based method remains a largely uncharted course, and, consequently, there is an unmeasured risk for all participants to engage in such decision making approaches.

On the other hand, there are also definite gains for each of the various prospective participants, especially with regard to scientific and technical components. What are the incentives for various actors to promote and participate in consensual approaches? In the following section, we will speculate on potential advantages and benefits as a step toward assessing the incentives of various groups to participate in such procedures. Table 5.2 summarizes the advantages and disadvantages of conventional and consensus-based methods for comparison. Although scientists do not represent an independent category of actors in public disputes, (since their involvement is usually predicated on an alignment with a stakeholding group or decision makers), our discussion in this chapter invites a consideration of their involvement in consensual procedures, since altering the role of science means the role of scientists will also change. Accordingly, we include forthwith, a discussion of the incentives for scientists to participate in consensual procedures.

Advantages to Decision Makers

For decision makers, consensus-based procedures offer several advantages with respect to how scientific and technical information is integrated into decisions and to the political legitimacy, control, and credibility of decision making. The benefits will vary, of course, according to the particular design of the consensus-based procedure.

First, if decision makers want to develop a clear understanding of relevant technical issues and options, consensus-based procedures can be an excellent approach. The process sets up incentives, like conventional procedures, for various stakeholders to volunteer relevant data and analysis as each party strives to shape and color the technical premises of the decision maker's ultimate decision. Massive amounts of information and expertise can be assembled quickly and at relatively little direct cost to the decision maker. Unlike conventional procedures, however, the interactive and iterative process enables the decision maker to set and enforce a standard for the presentation of information. Data can be requested in comparable formats to address specific questions, and obfuscatory language can be eliminated, especially with the assistance of a vigilant facilitator. As a result, decision makers are more likely to receive technical information in a form they find intelligible and will be better equipped to develop a technically sound decision.

Consensus-based procedures can also be used to generate a consensus on technical issues which may be appealing to decision makers wishing to avoid bickering over scientific uncertainties. When technical disputes are "resolved" (either by consensually invalidating all but one analysis or by acknowledging the validity of differing analyses), the decision maker can more readily move the discussion forward to the political interests at stake. In other words, stakeholders will less likely be able to hide their motives behind surrogate arguments on technical issues. The decision maker can thus gain a clearer understanding of the political interests and expend her

Table 5.2 Major Advantages and Disadvantages of Conventional and Consensus-Based Procedures for Policy Actors by Major Category

CONVENTIONAL PROCEDURES

POLICY ACTOR	Potential Advantages	Potential Disadvantages
Resource-Poor Stakeholders	Scientific disagreement can be used as aid for mobilizing political support	Lack technical expertise Lack resources to hire expertise Lack access to information (data, equipment, etc.) Lack entry into debate
Resource-Rich Stakeholders	Privileged access to data, analysis Can better absorb costs of drawn-out process Can launch expensive and sometimes effective media campaign	Even if eventual court win, preferred policy not necessarily implemented Stereotyped image stirs public disfavor
Decision Makers	Can cite scientific arguments to defend decision Decision making structure is in place Courts likely to rule in favor if decision is challenged on the basis of undeterminable scientific issues	Information incomplete and presentations confusing Limited communications Unknown degree of power conferred upon experts Credibility poor among dissatisfied stakeholders Distorted reading of policy preferences of groups Apparent concessions by others interpreted as favoritism
Scientists	Unique status awarded to scientists Consulting opportunities for scientists	Potential loss of public credibility for institution of science Advice can be disregarded by decision makers Pressure to reach "one answer"

energies toward integrating the interests into a viable agreement. A consensus on technical issues will also enable the decision maker to act more confidently, knowing that her decision is unlikely to be criticized as technically unsound, a condition that might later embarrass the decision maker.

With respect to political legitimacy, decision makers are often frustrated when painfully deliberated decisions are subsequently challenged and their implementation delayed. By definition, when consensus-based methods yield products, they are products that are politically acceptable and, usually, technically feasible. Unless stakeholders are satisfied, no agreement will be

CONSENSUS-BASED PROCEDURES

Potential Advantages

Share expertise through coalitions
Greater access to information
Ticket to entry not scientific expertise
Opportunity to express all concerns

Good public image
Greatest concerns more likely to be addressed
Higher certainty of outcome (can plan ahead)

Share information
Share expertise
Good public image
Wider array of interests heard
Richer understanding of various groups' interests
Better working relationships with groups involved
Scientifically unwise decisions avoided

Easier for individuals to change their mind if new evidence arises
Greater credibility if not seen as "hired gun"
More likely to be listened to
Brings together information from diverse sources

Potential Disadvantages

Consensus not good for political mobilization
Time-consuming
Delay as tactic is forfeited
Cannot exploit scientific uncertainty

Lose advantage of information and expertise
Cannot exploit scientific uncertainty
Delay as tactic is forfeited

Lose some discretionary decision making power
Requires concentrated dedication of time

More "conservative" science

reached. Importantly, consensual approaches do not necessarily fulfill all the demands of stakeholders. In the worst of cases, while perhaps no one is entirely satisfied with the all elements of the decision, a sufficient number of highly-ranked concerns is dealt with in an adequate manner so that the threshold for each group's approval is passed. It should be noted that approval from a particular group may result not from a minimal level of satisfaction with regard to the group's initial "wish list" of concerns, but from the group's assessment that the negotiated outcome is superior to the likely outcome under conventional decision making. (In negotiation jargon, the negotiated agreement is found preferable to a group's BATNA, or "best alternative to a negotiated agreement.") In the best of cases, agreements reached through consensual procedures constitute a full integration of competing stakeholding interests into a creative proposal. In any case, the group's accord, although not a guarantee, increases the probability that the decision will not be contested later in court and implementation and enforcement will proceed smoothly. In the wood stoves regulatory negotiation, participants went so far as to sign a statement promising to defend the rules (if EPA promulgated the rules as agreed upon during the negotiations) against future court challenges, should any arise.

Also, decision makers committed to facilitating meaningful participation for all stakeholders may be frustrated by conventional procedures that allow well-articulated disputes over scientific aspects of decisions to overshadow other issues and interests and result in the effective disenfranchisement of substantial segments of the stakeholding community. The subsequent dissent and disillusionment of such groups is potentially destabilizing both in terms of implementation of the decision itself and the decision maker's own political base. By defining participation to include the recognition of political interests rather than technical competence, consensus-based methods offer decision makers a means of receiving a broader array of viewpoints and an opportunity to accommodate these concerns in their decision choice. A consensual approach thus may be politically expedient for decision makers.

Decision makers concerned about maintaining choice in their decisions also reap a clear gain vis-a-vis scientists and technical experts. Consensus-based methods that enable participants to better comprehend scientific and technical aspects of decisions allow decision makers (and other participants) without technical expertise to recover a certain degree of control over the identification and choice of alternatives, which have become the domain of those most fluent in the technical complexities of a given problem. As decision makers develop a stronger understanding of technical arguments, they are able to evaluate and even devise new alternatives that are consistent with technical knowledge, their perception and ranking of competing interests, and their personal concerns. Scientists and technical experts remain as "advisors," but are appropriately restrained.

Finally, consensual approaches that involve stakeholders and scientists yield decisions that are likely to be more credible to both participants in the process and outsiders. The interests of stakeholders are not subordinated to the declarations of scientists or technical experts, but neither are political concerns placated at the expense of scientific or technical soundness. By helping to develop the decision maker's perceptive framework, stakeholders and the science community both come to a fuller appreciation of the decision maker's task and the ultimate decision. Again, credible decisions

Advantages for Stakeholders

Consensus-based methods offer attractive opportunities to stakeholders in public decisions, although the benefits do not come without serious costs. To begin with, the extent to which consensus-based approaches are "voluntary" is variable.[2] For example, a court order to negotiate a settlement is not truly a voluntary circumstance, given the potentially high cost of appearing uncooperative before the judge, who would otherwise render the decision. The decision to pursue a consensual approach also is usually carefully circumscribed. As in the EPA wood stoves case, the decision maker can retain a large degree of discretion by setting the initial agenda and marking the boundaries of negotiable items. In spite of such possible drawbacks, however, a decision maker's invitation to engage in a consensus-based procedure should not be lightly declined by parties desiring to influence a decision.

The advantages of consensus-based procedures to stakeholders will vary to some extent according to their position in the public discussion. As argued in the previous chapter, consensus-based procedures offer tremendous opportunities for traditionally resource-poor groups to strengthen their role in public decision making by enhancing their ability to deal with technical and scientific elements. Stakeholders who are not part of the technical debate and who have concerns not entertained by the advocates of positions linked to dominant technical debates may gain an opportunity to expand the range of issues and decision alternatives considered and addressed in the decision (at least to the extent that their concerns and interests may be inadvertently overlooked and not intentionally ignored by decision makers).

The very act of participating in the deliberations that lead to a decision can provide valuable learning benefits, especially to groups that are traditionally more distant from the decision making locus. The discussions that occur in a consensual procedure will convey not only technical information to negotiators, but also insights into the priorities of the decision maker and competing stakeholding groups. Such knowledge can be used immediately to devise proposals that are more likely to be accepted by others and can be held and constructively applied in future confrontations.

Finally, participation in consensus-based procedures can increase the visibility of otherwise marginal stakeholding groups and contribute to the legitimization and acceptance of their concerns in public discussions over the long-term. Although involvement in public discourse at any forum will provide opportunities for groups to place new issues into the public consciousness, and some of the more overtly adversarial channels may even provide greater exposure for the issues, a consensus-based procedure may be more effective in certain instances. A participant in a regulatory negotiation convened by the Federal Trade Commission, for example, thought the negotiations improved the manufacturers' understanding of how existing policies affect consumers and how to better handle complaints about their products (Singer). In spite of the failure of the negotiations to produce a new federal rule, the consensus-based procedure may have resulted in actual changes in the relationship between these two adversarial parties and practical gains for both.

In light of the apparent gains for traditionally resource-poor groups to engage in consensus-based methods, what incentives exist for traditionally dominant groups, such as business and industry? Why should they engage in a procedure that requires them to share technical information and expertise that they might manipulate to their advantage under conventional procedures?

A popular image of business and industry is that they typically hold deep bank accounts that can be tapped to fund self-serving technical studies and expert testimonies. They, in fact, often do have direct and exclusive access to a vast vault of information and expertise. Even manufacturers in small industries, like the wood stove producers, have on the payroll persons with engineering expertise to assist in the research and development of their products. Patently, it is their business to gather technical data about their product and its production. Leading manufacturers of large industries, like the petrochemical industry, have proprietary data concerning the chemical substances utilized in their production processes. They also keep health records on employees and, in many cases, have in their hands rare data on the health conditions of employees exposed to dangerous chemicals. In terms of access to data and expertise, the ability of industry often greatly exceeds even that of regulating agencies including the Environmental Protection Agency and the Occupational Safety and Health Administration.

However, not all firms are as resource-rich as those appearing on the "Fortune 500" list. Moreover, the concerns of different firms within an industry are rarely identical. Partly as a result of the stereotyped image of "big business" and "corporate giants," however, the scientific arguments of business and industry involved in contested public decisions are often taken lightly by decision makers simply because they are presumed to purposely withhold and distort information to abet the firm's or industry's single-minded, avaricious mission to prosper. The subtleties of the firm or industry's multifaceted and diverse needs are often blurred, and missed by decision makers considering competing political claims.

Furthermore, under conventional decision making, corporations (and non-business interests) compete on an "all or nothing" basis. Accordingly, one's scientific arguments are either "right" or "wrong." Winning on the scientific front, however, does not mean winning the battle. As the *South Terminal v. EPA* case cited in Chapter 1 illustrates, in judicial challenges to administrative decisions, a court will rule in favor of the plaintiff only if the analysis of the agency is found to be clearly in error. Even then, however, a ruling in favor of the plaintiff at best only means remanding the decision back to the agency for further review. Corporate stakeholders can find themselves expending considerable time and money on legal challenges for dubious gains.

In consensus-based procedures, industry spokespersons and representatives from individual firms gain an opportunity to differentiate themselves from one another and to dispel many traditional stereotypes and misconceptions. In the wood stoves regulatory negotiation, for example, small stove manufacturers held separate representation from the industry trade group, which they believed was dominated by the largest producers. During the negotiations, it indeed became apparent that proposed regulations would affect the production schedules and costs of small producers differently than those of the large manufacturers, and minor modifications were made to equalize the impacts.

Consensus-based procedures also enhance the credibility of scientific and technical information industry groups contribute. Not only is information routinely subject to critical review, but since there is a mutual understanding among the group that technical parameters do not determine policy choices, participants are less inclined to casually dismiss submissions from any source.

Through participation in consensus-based procedures, industry stakeholders also gain a sense of what the ultimate decision will look like. In the business world where "time is money," companies often assign high value to predictability in the regulatory environment. For similar reasons, many stakeholders may prefer processes that produce decisions that are likely to be implemented. Contested decisions can create delays and even policy reversals, which can incur great costs for business. Put simply, corporate competitors may do well to trade what may be lesser gains for greater certainty.

Moreover, just as resource-poor groups can strengthen their voices through forming coalitions, better-endowed industry groups may also pool resources with allies within the negotiating group. A participant representing a major automobile manufacturer in an EPA regulatory negotiation commented, "[F]or the first time, my competitors and I were part of a team. Rather than trying to outsmart each other, we had to consider each other's needs as part of an industry group." (Singer, p. 147). A policy option created jointly by groups working together is far more likely to integrate a broader array of concerns, which can be politically attractive to a decision maker.

Finally, participating in a consensus-based procedure that aims to produce a technically sound decision that meets the interests of the decision maker as well as other participants will help to build a positive public image for business and industry stakeholders. Rather than projecting images of self-interested bullies who attempt to buy off or manipulate decision makers or who launch expensive court challenges if an unfavored decision alternative is chosen, business and industry groups that participate in a consensual process will appear reasonable and public-spirited. Consensus-based methods thus offer distinct advantages even to the "giants" in the public arena.

Advantages for Scientists

Scientists in public disputes are usually not independent stakeholders. More often, they are drawn into public debates as advisors to other stakeholders or the decision maker(s). When they enter on their own accord, and do not quickly ally with one of the contending groups, one may then presume they hold a separate interest in the decision in question. In such a case, they can be considered a "stakeholder," but one whose incentives to participate in a consensus-based supplement are distinct from those of other stakeholding groups. Whatever the case, as a party to a dispute or as an advisor, scientists can either balk or buy into a proposal to undertake a consensual procedure, and it is important to consider the incentives for scientists to participate in such activities.

Scientists initially may feel reluctant to join a process in which they fear they will lose some control over the interpretation of their work. Consensus-based procedures that aim to involve all policy actors (stakeholders, decision makers, and scientists) in establishing the technical basis of public decisions may appear to force a compromise of scientific methodology by opening it to political bargaining among non-scientist stakeholders. On the contrary, scientists participating in consensual procedures need not feel pressured into supporting opinions with which they do not agree. In fact, in several ways, scientists can more easily maintain their chosen roles as "seekers of truth" (rather than "advocates of policy") in consensus-based procedures.

First, consensus-based procedures encourage a thorough examination and, sometimes, further data collection and analysis of scientific issues. As discussed earlier, at any given point, scientific knowledge on a specific question is partial and incomplete. The evidence and arguments put forth by a particular scientist (or group of scientists) represent just one piece of a larger puzzle. In adversarial procedures, scientists are asked to defend their work. In a consensual procedure, by contrast, scientists with different views are asked to debate the relative validity and significance of their work toward a common objective, to determine exactly what they can and cannot agree on. This shared goal potentially creates a rich opportunity for scientists to synthesize divergent data into a new theory or a composite understanding of the issue in question. Integrating new data into existing theories or modifying theories to account for new information is an important aspect of how, ideally, scientific inquiry advances the state of knowledge.

Moreover, under conventional, adversarial procedures scientists frequently feel bound (formally through payroll links or informally through their strong, public association with particular policy alternatives) by their original arguments. A consensual procedure that separates political stakes from scientific contests affords scientists greater flexibility to "change their minds," if new information persuades them to do so. In this sense, a consensual procedure frees individual scientists to act more as the "ideal scientist," especially those who are called into a public debate by their employer or research sponsor.

Third, consensus-based procedures educate non-expert policy actors to develop appropriate expectations about the capability of scientific expertise in public decision making. Observing scientists debate and defend conflicting viewpoints can be highly instructive to non-expert policy actors. Even while their understanding of substantive details may remain somewhat vague, they are able to gain a feel for the complexity of the issue, and the limits to current knowledge. When stakeholders and decision makers learn to appreciate the multiple perspectives possible in viewing a particular issue, and the value of each one, they are less likely to demand consistency or uniformity of opinion from scientific advisors. Non-expert policy actors (and the public in general) will be less inclined to demand single answers that scientists are not able to provide at the moment. Under such conditions, scientists will be able to speak more freely with conviction about what they do know. As a result, non-expert policy actors are less likely to believe the scientists are acting out of political or material self-interest, and the general credibility of science as an institution will also be protected.

Finally, while credibility is important, alone it is insufficient to ensure that the advice of scientists will be heeded by the other policy actors. In consensual procedures, the participation of scientists in the formulation of policy alternatives gives scientists a direct hand in helping to shape the ultimate decision. In this way, they can help to make certain that the decision is consistent with their understanding of the current state of scientific knowledge. Moreover, they can guide decision makers toward initiating actions that will help to fill gaps in the current state of knowledge (by including monitoring provisions, further data collection, or continuing analysis as part of their decisions on controversial projects in which scientific uncertainty impedes a more precise understanding of the consequences of decision alternatives, for example).

For all stakeholders, an invitation to participate in consensus-based procedures offers an opportunity to act proactively in a public decision rather than reactively. That is, in contrast to conventional procedures, such as public comment periods or public hearings that involve stakeholding groups after a tentative policy choice is already formulated, consensus-based procedures are commonly instituted before a proposal is developed. Regulatory negotiations occur before the drafting of preliminary rules by an agency; policy dialogues are held in advance of policy decisions. All else being equal, the earlier a party becomes involved in a decision making process, the greater the potential for their influencing the formulation of the options and the ultimate decision choice.

Should We Use Consensual Procedures?

Public decisions imply a redistribution of resources (be they material, economic, or political in nature). In a highly diversified society that is culturally pluralistic, economically stratified, and politically conflictual, such redistributions are inevitably contentious. Decision making that does not address political concerns will ultimately fail to endure. Inasmuch as individual public decisions represent only a tactical truce among contending groups battling over resources, preserving the preeminence of political interests in public decision making is critical.

Under existing institutional structures, science is often used as a weapon to dominate public decisions. Scientific and technical resources are not distributed evenly throughout society. Highly educated individuals have greater access than those with fewer formal credentials and much scientific activity is sponsored, directed, and held in private hands. This has implications for both those who have current access to information and expertise, as well as for how the agenda for scientific research evolved and how the base of scientific knowledge developed. Even "public" science, i.e., funded by government, is heavily skewed toward particular fields and project areas, for example, toward those with potential military applications. As a result, the scientific base for production-oriented technologies is far more sophisticated than our understanding of the coincidental, environmental and health effects of such technologies.

Public decision making procedures that foster adversarial uses of scientific argumentation can be suspected of systematically favoring economically powerful groups. Decision making methods that deemphasize the persuasive power of scientific argumentation represents a step toward equalizing the opportunity for groups to compete for public resources. If equality of opportunity in public decision making is valued, defusing scientific "weapons" may be a critical element of public decision making procedures, second only to prescriptions for broad public participation.

These findings suggest that consensus-based procedures can result in favorable transformations in the role of science that lead toward more participatory and democratic public decision making. Specifically, scientific knowledge can be useful for stakeholders and decision makers in appraising the scientific soundness and political desirability of decision alternatives from their own perspective, rather than as a weapon that disguises the politics of decision making. This less adversarial role will move decision making toward scientifically sound decisions without sacrificing democratic principles.

In addition, consensual procedures not only facilitate an understanding of scientific factors and a clarification of technical disagreement, they also encourage discussion of the political interests behind public debates. A far more integrative discussion of science and politics, and the politics of scientific arguments, results.

A consensus-based procedure by definition must be voluntary, however. For groups contending in contests over public decisions, consensus-based procedures ought to be viewed as one of a package of tactical options available. The choice of political tactics in science-intensive decision making depends on a group's scientific and technical resources, as well as political and contextual factors. Before agreeing to participate in a consensus-based procedure, each prospective participant ought to consider three critical factors: (1) the advantages and disadvantages of a consensus-based approach given a group's resources, (2) a comparison of likely outcomes under all decision making path options, and (3) the compatibility of the objectives of a consensus-based procedure with the political objectives of the stakeholder's involvement in the particular controversy.

A decision to engage in a consensus-based procedure ought to begin first with an analysis of the advantages and disadvantages that consensus-based approaches offer. The previous section of this chapter identified the advantages of consensus-based procedures; we review here some of the more prominent ones. Resource-poor groups fight an uphill battle regardless of the front on which confrontation occurs, but these groups, which frequently lack access to technical information and expertise, can be severely handicapped when a debate is focused on technical aspects. Conversely, resource-rich adversaries possess substantial advantage with regard to persuading decision makers and the public of the scientific soundness of their preferred policy positions. In these situations, consensus-based procedures that offer a sharing of technical information and expertise can constitute a tactical coup for resource-poor groups.

In comparison to resource-poor groups, resource-rich groups have a relative advantage under both consensus-based and conventional decision making. The measure of whether such a group should participate in a consensus-based procedure is not only whether its preferred policy option will prevail over those of resource-poor adversaries, but how the group will obtain its objectives and at what cost. A land developer who negotiates with abutting land owners and other community representatives is likely to encounter less resistance at subsequent points in the processing of permit applications and construction than one who wins the first battle in a feisty courtroom. A developer who gains approval for a project after the concerns of the community have been aired and addressed by appropriate alterations to a project's design is also likely to continue to reap valuable rewards in the future resulting from a positive community reputation.

Decision makers appear to have much to gain and little to lose by suggesting consensus-based supplements in decision making that involves complex scientific and technical issues. Enhancement of the political acceptability, credibility, scientific and technical soundness, and technical feasibility of consensually-derived decisions are not inconsequential benefits. The highest cost may actually boil down to the concentrated dedication of time required of decision makers themselves, or credible representatives.

The second factor that ought to be considered before agreeing to participate in a consensus-based procedure is an analysis of the likely outcomes under all decision making process options. In negotiation jargon, this amounts to assessing one's BATNA, or "best alternative to a negotiated agreement."[3] In brief, if a group's alternatives to participation appear favorable, that group should feel little inclination to engage in a consensus-based procedure. Conversely, if alternatives to a consensus-based procedure (such as a unilateral decision by a public official or a court decision) appear unlikely to serve the interests of a particular group well, that group should recognize greater incentives to experiment with new procedures. Although the outcome of a conventional procedure is less predictable at some times than at others, some contextual factors are sufficiently well-understood to send strong signals.

In a political climate led by a federal administration that believes the highest priority should be to protect the environment, for example, environmental advocates may believe their interests will be better promoted under conventional administrative and judicial patterns of decision making, where government retains considerable discretion. Under such conditions, there is little urgency to pursue alternative paths. On the other hand, under an anti-environment leadership that has set out to castrate existing programs and dismember federal environmental policies, a strategy to pursue incremental, rather than radical gains, may be preferable to environmental advocates, and a consensus-based procedure may be one means of doing so.

Pursuing a procedure that is supplementary to conventional decision making also means that conventional decision making options may change as a result. The calculation of the expected outcome of a conventional decision making process that has been disrupted by a consensus-based procedure that failed to produce an agreement is complicated and somewhat uncertain. It is still unclear how a court would look upon a legal challenge initiated by a party who has withdrawn from earlier negotiations, especially in a multi-party dispute in which other parties had wished to continue negotiations. Part of the risk of agreeing to participate in a consensus-based procedure, then, is the impact a failed attempt may have on the outcome of the conventional decision making process. In the Michigan fishing case, the Bay Mills tribe subsequently withdrew their support of the negotiated agreement, and a court trial was conducted on the merits of the negotiated agreement. The judge ruled against the tribe's legal challenge.

The final factor that each party ought to consider is an obvious one, but one that is easily overlooked. Whether or not a group ought to enter a consensus-based procedure is a derivative of the political objective of that group's involvement in a particular debate. In some cases, a group may deliberately exploit scientific uncertainty in order to draw public attention to a particular issue or decision. A consensual procedure that will clarify the basis of disagreement, even if it illuminates differences in political interests or values in the process, may not serve as effectively to capture the public's imagination, interest, support, and sympathy as other methods of political activism, such as street demonstrations or lengthy court battles that center on advocacy uses of science. As a tool for political mobilization, the symbolic usefulness of disputing sometimes outweighs the benefits of finding a resolution.

Also, consensus-based procedures presume a desire for forward movement. If delaying a decision is a primary objective of a group, (as a tactic, such as for causing an opposing party to incur additional expenses or to delay the formal decision until after political elections), engaging in a consensus-based procedure only to prolong the decision making process is likely only to aggravate other participants who eventually realize the group's real motives. An uncooperative group, or one that ultimately sabotages a consensus-based effort by premeditatedly withdrawing, is likely to suffer some kind of backlash. If delaying a decision serves the best interest of a group, the group probably ought to avoid consensus-based procedures altogether.

As a last note, a group may believe that its demands are non-negotiable. For example, a group may believe that a stringent health standard is more important than an achievable one as a statement of the government's commitment to protecting public health.[4] Or, a group opposing the construction of a nuclear power plant may see no possibility of meeting their own primary interest while addressing the concerns of the plant developer. In such cases, these groups should choose (wisely) to avoid consensus-based procedures. As Susskind and Cruikshank have noted, disputes seen as distributional in nature, contests over who gets what, are amenable to consensus-based procedures (Susskind and Cruikshank), but when groups are battling over whether and not how something occurs or over defining a fundamental principle, expending time and energy clarifying the scientific or technical elements of the dispute will not move the disputants closer to agreement.

If, however, a group wants a decision to be made, or believes one is imminent, an invitation to join a consensus-based procedure can represent an unequalled opportunity to shape that decision. In particular, a less contentious use of science developed through a consensual process enables groups not otherwise well-equipped to battle on the turf of experts to compete for control of public resources. While the playing field may not be level, the rules in consensus-based procedures may well provide far greater opportunity for fair play than conventional public decision processes in those arenas of public decision making in which scientific argumentation is typically prominent. For a technologically sophisticated society overall, consensus-based procedures may be just the key needed to open the door to scientifically-wise, participatory decision making.

Notes

1. See Lowi's, *The End of Liberalism*.

2. The voluntary nature of consensus-based procedures is a cornerstone of a participant's base of negotiating power since negotiation scholars often write of BATNA, or a negotiator's alternative, as a central part of a negotiator's power.

3. See Fisher and Ury's, *Getting to Yes*.

4. One should understand clearly the real costs of such public statements, however. A lower standard that is met may be of greater immediate benefit to public health than a higher standard that is not enforced. On the other hand, setting unreachable goals sends a signal that can inspire more radical action, ultimately leading to greater overall benefits.

Appendix 1: Interviews

New York City MSW Incinerator Case

Personal Interview

Barry Commoner, Director, Center for the Biology of Natural Systems, Queens College, Flushing, New York, October, 1986.

Telephone Interview

Marc David Block, New York Academy of Sciences, several during September 1986.

EPA Wood Stoves Regulatory Negotiation

Telephone Interviews

Robert Ajax, Environmental Protection Agency, Chief of Standards Development Branch, Air Office, May 21, 1987.
William Becker, State and Territorial Air Pollution Program Administrators (STAPPA) and Association of Local Air Pollution Control Officials (ALAPCO), May 12, 1987.
Larry Canaday, Woodcutters Manufacturing, June 12, 1987.
John Charles, Oregon Environmental Council, May 1987.
Richard Colyer, Environmental Protection Agency, Standards Development Branch, May 7, 1987.
Donnis Corn, a-b Fabricators, Inc., May 18, 1987.
David Doniger, Natural Resources Defense Council, May 1987.
Harold Garabedian, State of Vermont, Air Pollution Control Program, Agency of Environmental Conservation, June 2, 1987.
R.D. Gros Jean, Corning Glass, May 12, 1987.
Brad Hollomon, New York State Energy Research and Development Authority, May 12, 1987.
Jim King, State of Colorado, Department of Health, May 13, 1987.
John Kowalczyk, State of Oregon, Department of Environmental Quality, May 11, 1987.
Neil Martin, Brugger Exports, Ltd., June 1, 1987.
David Menotti, Wood Heating Alliance, May 5, 1987.
Jay W. Shelton, Shelton Research, Inc., May 11, 1987.

Personal Interviews

Doreen Cantor, Environmental Protection Agency, Enforcement and Compliance Division, Washington, D.C., May 1, 1987.
Philip Harter, Washington, D.C., May 1, 1987.
David Swankin, Consumer's Federation of America, Washington, D.C., May 1, 1987.

Michigan Fishing Dispute

Telephone Interviews

Richard Clark, Institute for Fisheries Research, August 27, 1987.
Robert Doherty, professor of history, University of Pittsburgh, September 1, 1987.
William Eger, biologist, Chippewa-Ottawa Fishery Management Authority, August 14, 1987.
Daniel Green, attorney for Sault St. Marie tribe of Chippewa Indians, August 12, 1987.
Nino Green, attorney for non-tribal commercial fishers, August 17, 1987.
Bruce Greene, attorney for Bay Mills Indian Community, August 13, 17, and 19, 1987.
Wilbur Hartman, biologist, U.S. Department of Interior, August 21, 1987.
Richard Hatch, Great Lakes Fishery Laboratory, Fish and Wildlife Service, U.S. Department of Interior, August 20, 1987.
Francis McGovern, professor, University of Alabama, July 1987.
Francine Rabinowitz, July 20, 1987.
William Rastetter, attorney for Grand Traverse Band of Chippewa-Ottawa Indians, August 19, 1987.
Stephen Schultz, attorney, Grand Traverse Area Sport Fishing Association, Michigan Charterboat Association, Michigan Steelhead and Salmon Fisherman's Association, August 13, 1987.
Mariana Shulstad, Department of Interior, August 17, 1987.
Ronald Skoog, former director of Michigan Department of Natural Resources, September 21, 1987.
Peter Stekettee, attorney, Michigan United Conservation Clubs, August 14, 1987.
Elizabeth Valentine, former Michigan Assistant Attorney General, August 14, 1987.
Asa Wright, biologist, Michigan Department of Natural Resources, Fisheries Division, August 20, 1987.

Appendix 2: Participants in EPA WBS Negotiated Rulemaking

Negotiators/Affiliation

1. Robert Ajax, U.S. EPA
2. William Becker, STAPPA/ALAPCO*
3. Larry Canaday, Woodcutters Mfg.
4. John Charles, Oregon Environmental Council
5. Donnis Corn, a-b Fabricators, Inc.
6. David Doniger, Natural Resources Defense Council, Inc.
7. Harold Garabedian, Vermont Air Pollution Control Program
8. Robert Geiter, Applied Ceramics
9. R. D. Gros Jean, Corning Class Works
10. Brad Holloman, New York State Energy Research and Development Authority and New York State Energy Office
11. Jim King, Colorado Department of Health
12. John Kowalczyk, Oregon Department of Environmental Quality
13. Neil Martin, Brugger Exports, Ltd.
14. David Menotti, Wood Heating Alliance
15. Jay W. Shelton, Shelton Research, Inc.
16. David Swankin, Consumer Federation of America

Facilitator

Phil Harter, Esq., Consultant to EPA

---

*State and Territorial Air Pollution Program Administrators and Association of Local Air Pollution Control Officials

Source: *Federal Register*, Vol. 52, No. 32, February 18, 1978.

Executive Secretary

Chris Kirtz, U.S. EPA

Observers

Wayne Leiss, Office of Management and Budget
George J. Lippert, U.S. Forest Service
Jean Vernet, U.S. Department of Energy

Bibliography

Abrams, Nancy Ellen, and R. Stephen Berry. 1977. "Mediation: A Better Alternative to Science Courts." *Bulletin of the Atomic Scientists.* 33: 50-53.

Albury, Randall. 1982. "The Politics of Truth: A Social Interpretation of Scientific Knowledge, with an Application to the Case of Sociobiology," in Michael Ruse, ed. *Nature Animated.* Dordrecht, Holland: D. Reidel.

Amy, Douglas. 1987. *The Politics of Environmental Mediation.* New York: Columbia University Press.

Ashford, Nicholas A. 1984. "Advisory Committees in OSHA and EPA: Their Use in Regulatory Decisionmaking," *Science, Technology, and Human Values.* 9(1): 72-82.

Bacow, Lawrence. 1980. "The Technical and Judgmental Dimensions of Impact Assessment," *Environmental Impact Assessment Review.* 1(2): 109-124.

Bacow, Lawrence, and Michael Wheeler. 1984. *Environmental Dispute Resolution.* New York: Plenum Press.

Barnes, Barry, and David Edge. 1982. *Science in Context.* Cambridge, MA: MIT Press.

Barry, Donald B., and Howard R. Whitcomb. 1981. *The Legal Foundations of Public Administration.* St. Paul, MN: West Publishing Co.

Ben-David, Joseph. 1971. *The Scientist's Role in Society.* New Jersey: Prentice-Hall.

Bingham, Gail. 1986. *Resolving Environmental Disputes: A Decade of Experience.* Washington, D.C.: The Conservation Foundation.

Boffey, Philip. 1975. *The Brain Bank of America.* New York: McGraw-Hill.

Brickman, Ronald. 1984. "Science and the Politics of Toxic Chemical Regulation: U.S. and European Contrasts," *Science, Technology, and Human Values.* 9(1): 107-111.

Brooks, Harvey. 1980. "Stratospheric Ozone, the Scientific Community and Public Policy," in Frank A. Bower and Richard B. Ward, eds. *Stratospheric Ozone and Man, Volume II.* Boca Raton, Florida: CRC Press.

_____. 1984. "The Resolution of Technically-Intensive Public Policy Disputes," *Science, Technology, and Human Values.* 9(1): 39-50.

_____. 1988. "Controlling Technology: Risks, Costs, and Benefits," in Michael E. Kraft and Norman J. Vig, eds. *Technology and Politics.* Durham, N.C.: Duke University Press.

Burger, Edward J. 1980. *Science at the White House.* Baltimore: The Johns Hopkins Press.

Cigler, Allan J., and Burdett A. Loomis. 1983. "Introduction: The Changing Nature of Interest Group Politics," in Allan J. Cigler and Burdett A. Loomis, eds. *Interest Group Politics*. Washington, D.C.: CQ Press.

Citizens Advisory Committee for Resource Recovery in Brooklyn. 1981. *Request for Qualifications/Request for Proposals.* December 31, 1981.

City of New York, Department of Sanitation. 1984. *Draft Environmental Impact State (DEIS) for the Proposed Resource Recovery facility at the Brooklyn Navy Yard.* New York: Department of Sanitation. Office of Resource Recovery.

———. 1984. *Draft Environmental Impact State (DEIS) for the Proposed Resource Recovery Facility at the Brooklyn Navy Yard. Executive Summary.* New York: Department of Sanitation. Office of Resource Recovery.

Clean Air Act, U.S. Code, vol. 42, 1967.

Cobb, Roger W., and Charles D. Elder. 1972. *Participation in American Politics: The Dynamics of Agenda-Building.* Baltimore and London: The Johns Hopkins University Press.

Collingridge, David. 1980. *The Social Control of Technology.* New York: St. Martin's Press.

Commoner, Barry. 1985. "Incinerators: The City's Half-Baked and Hazardous Solution to the Solid-Waste Problem," *New York Affairs.* 9(2): 19–33.

———. 1972. *The Closing Circle: Nature, Man and Technology.* New York: Knopf.

Commoner, Barry, Michael McNamara, Karen Shapiro, and Thomas Webster. 1984. *Environmental and Economic Analysis of Alternative Municipal Solid Waste Disposal Technologies—Vol. I: An Assessment of the Risks Due to Emissions of Chlorinated Dioxins and Dibenzofurans from Proposed New York City Incinerators (May 1); Vol. II: The Origins of Chlorinated Dioxins and Dibenzofurans Emitted by Incinerators That Burn Unseparated Municipal Solid Waste, and an Assessment of Methods of Controlling Them (December 1); Vol. III: A Comparison of Different Estimates of the Risk Due to Emissions of Chlorinated Dioxins and Dibenzofurans from Proposed New York City Incinerators (Including a Critique of the Hart Report) (December 1); and Vol. IV: Summary (December 1).* Flushing, NY: Center for the Biology of Natural Systems, Queens College, CUNY.

Cormick, Gerald W., and Alana Knaster. 1986. "Mediation and Scientific Issues," *Environment.* 28(10): 6ff.

Crandall, Robert W., and Lester B. Lave, eds. 1981. *The Scientific Basis of Health and Safety Regulation.* Washington, D.C.: The Brookings Institution.

Dickson, David. 1984. *The New Politics of Science.* New York: Pantheon Books.

Doherty, Robert. 1985. *Troubled Waters: The Political Economy of Treaty-Right Fishing in Michigan's Great Lakes.* Unpublished manuscript.

Douglas, Mary, and Aaron Wildavsky. 1982. *Risk and Culture.* Berkeley, CA: University of California Press.

Ethyl Corporation v. EPA. 541 F.2d (D.C. Cir. 1976) (en banc), cert. denied. 426 U.S. 941 (1977).

Federal Register. Vol. 50, No. 149, Friday, August 2, 1985.

———. Vol. 51, No. 26, February 7, 1986.

Finkel, Adam M. 1988. "Dioxin: Are We Safer Now Than Before?" *Risk Analysis.* 8(2): 161–165.

Fischer, Carl William. 1966. "Scientists and Statesmen: A Profile of the Organization of the President's Science Advisory Committee," in Sanford A. Lakoff, ed. 1966. *Knowledge and Power.* New York: The Free Press.

Fisher, Roger, and William Ury. 1981. *Getting to Yes.* Boston, MA: Houghton Miflin Company.

Freedman, James O. 1978. *Crisis and Legitimacy.* New York: Cambridge University Press.

Fritschler, A. Lee. 1983. *Smoking and Politics: Policymaking and the Federal Bureaucracy.* 3rd edition. Englewood Cliffs, NJ: Prentice-Hall, Inc.

Green, Nino. 1983. *Brief in Support of Supplemental Petition to Intervene.* Filed in United States District Court, Western District of Michigan, Northern Division, in *U.S. v. Michigan,* November 1983.

Greenberg, Daniel S. 1969. *The Politics of Pure Science.* New York: New American Library.

Greenfield, Liah. 1987. "Science and National Greatness in 17th Century England," *Minerva.* XXV(1-2): 107–122.

Gusfield, Joseph. 1981. *The Culture of Public Problems.* Chicago: University of Chicago Press.

Gusman, Sam. 1981. "Policy Dialogue," *Environmental Comment.* November 1981: 14–16.

Hart, Fred C. and Associates, Inc. 1984. *Assessment of Potential Public Health Impacts Associated With Predicted Emissions of Polychlorinated Dibenzo-Dioxins (PCDD) and Polychlorinated Dibenzo-Furans (PCDF) From the Brooklyn Navy Yard Resource Recovery Facility.* New York: New York City Department of Sanitation.

Harter, Philip J. 1983. "The Political Legitimacy and Judicial Review of Consensual Rules," *The American University Law Review.* 32: 471–496.

———. 1986. "Regulatory Negotiation: An Overview," *Dispute Resolution Forum.* January 1986.

Hiskes, Anne L. and Richard P. Hiskes. 1986. *Science, Technology, and Policy Decisions.* Boulder, CO: Westview Press.

Hubbard, Ruth. 1990. *The Politics of Women's Biology.* New Brunswick, NJ: Rutgers University Press.

Kantrowitz, Arthur. 1967. "Proposal for an Institution for Scientific Judgment," *Science.* 156(3776): 765–764.

Konheim and Ketcham, Inc. 1985. *Evaluation of Risk of Dioxins and Furans From the Proposed Brooklyn Navy Yard Resource Recovery Facility.* Prepared with assistance from the Environmental Science Laboratory at Mt. Sinai School of Medicine. March 1985. Brooklyn, New York: Konheim and Ketcham.

Knelman, Fred H., ed. 1971. *1984 and All That.* Belmont, CA: Wadsworth Publishing Company, Inc.

Knorr-Cetina, Karin D. 1982. "Scientific Communities of Transepistemic Arenas of Research? A Critique for Quasi-Economic Models of Science," *Social Studies of Science.* 12(1): 101–130.

Konkel, R. Steven. 1987. "Dioxin Emissions and Trash-to-Energy Plants in New York City," *Environmental Impact Assessment Review.* 7(1): 37–55.

Kuhn, Thomas. 1962. *The Structure of Scientific Revolutions.* Berkeley: University of California Press.

——— . 1982. "Normal Measurement and Reasonable Judgment," in Barry Barnes and David Edge, eds. *Science in Context.* Cambridge, MA: The MIT Press.

Lakoff, Sanford A., ed. 1966. *Knowledge and Power.* New York: The Free Press.

Lapp, Ralph E. 1965. *The New Priesthood: The Scientific Elite and the Uses of Power.* New York: Harper & Row.

Latour, Bruno. 1979. *Life in the Laboratory.* Beverly Hills: Sage Publications.

Legal Times. April 22, 1985, "Master Lands Settlement that Almost Got Away."

Levanthal, Harold. 1974. "Environmental Decisionmaking and the Role of the Courts," *University of Pennsylvania Law Review.* 122(3): 509–555.

Lewicki, Roy J., and Joseph A. Litterer. 1985. *Negotiation.* Homewood, IL: Richard D. Irwin, Inc.

Little, Timothy G. 1984. "Court-Appointed Special Masters in Complex Environmental Litigation: City of Quincy v. Metropolitan District Commission," *Harvard Environmental Law Review.* 8: 395–475.

Longino, Helen. 1983. "Beyond 'Bad' Science: Skeptical Reflections on the Value-Freedom of Scientific Inquiry," *Science, Technology, and Human Values.* 8(1): 7–17.

Lowi, Theodore. 1969. *The End of Liberalism.* New York: W.W. Norton.

Majone, Giandomenico. 1984. "Science and Trans-Science in Standard Setting," *Science, Technology, and Human Values.* 9(1): 15–22.

Marcus, Alfred A. 1988. "Risk, Uncertainty, and Scientific Judgement," *Minerva,* 26(2): 138–152.

Mazur, Allan. 1973. "Disputes Between Experts." *Minerva.* 11: 243–262.

——— . 1981. *The Dynamics of Technical Controversy.* Washington, D.C.: Communications Press, Inc.

McCarthy, Jane with Alice Shorett. 1984. *Negotiating Settlements: A Guide to Environmental Mediation.* New York: American Arbitration Association.

McGovern, Francis E. 1986. "Toward a Functional Approach for Managing Complex Litigation," *University of Chicago Law Review.* 53: 440–493.

Melnick, R. Shep. 1983. *Regulation and the Courts: The Case of the Clean Air Act.* Washington, D.C.: The Brookings Institute.

Mernitz, Scott. 1980. *Mediation of Environmental Disputes: A Sourcebook.* New York: Praeger Publishers.

Merryman, Walter. Interview on the MacNeil-Lehrer News Hour, October 1988.

Mokken, R.J., and F.N. Stokman. 1976. "Power and Influence as Political Phenomena," in Brian Barry, ed. *Power and Political Theory.* New York: John Wiley.

Mulkay, Michael. 1979. *Science and the Sociology of Knowledge.* London: George Allen & Unwin.

Mullins, Nicholas. 1981. "Power, Social Structure, and Advice in American Science and the United States National Advisory System, 1958–1972," *Science, Technology, and Human Values.* 7(3): 4–19.

National Environmental Policy Act, Public Law 91-190 (1969), *U.S. Code,* vol. 42, Section 4331 *et seq.*

National Research Council, Committee on the Biological Effects of Ionizing Radiations. *The Effect on Populations of Exposure to Low Levels of Ionizing Radiation: 1980.* Washington, D.C.: National Academy Press.

Natural Resources Defense Council, Inc. v. EPA, D.C. Cir. No. 7202233, October 28, 1973.
Nelkin, Dorothy. 1975. "The Political Impact of Technical Expertise," *Social Studies of Science*. 5:35-54.
———, ed. 1984. *Controversy: Politics of Technical Decisions*. (2nd ed.) Beverly Hills and London: Sage Publications.
Nelkin, Dorothy, and Pollack. 1981. *The Atom Beseiged*. Cambridge, MA: MIT Press.
New York Academy of Sciences. 1984(a). "Resource Recovery in New York City: Science-Intensive Public Policy Issues, A Facilitated Public-Policy Dialogue." Summary of proceedings. New York: New York Academy of Sciences.
———. 1984(b). Audio tape recording of "Resource Recovery in New York City: Science-Intensive Public Policy Issues, A Facilitated Public-Policy Dialogue." December 18, 1984.
New York City, Department of Sanitation. 1984(a). *Draft Environmental Impact Statement for the Proposed Resource Recovery Facility at the Brooklyn Navy Yard* and cover letter.
———. 1984(b). *The Waste Disposal Problem in New York City: A Proposal for Action*.
New York Times, October 15, 1984, "Time to Burn the Trash"; November 17, 1984, "Reducing New York Trash"; November 26, 1984, "Is New York City's Incinerator Plan a Health Threat?"; December 7, 1984, "Officials Fault Plan to Build 8 Trash Plants"; December 20, 1984, "Don't Fiddle; Burn New York's Trash"; December 21, 1984, "Board of Estimate Approves Plan for 5 Incinerators in City"; December 25, 1984, "The Vote on Incinerators: Politics and a City Board"; January 5, 1985, "How to Hedge Our Dioxin Bet"; July 8, 1985, "Waste No More Time on Waste"; August 14, 1985, "Disputed Incinerator Plan for Brooklyn Navy Yard Near Vote"; August 15, 1985, "A Two-Pronged War on NYC Waste"; August 15, 1985, "When the Trash Can't Be Buried"; August 16, 1985, "Approval Is Given for Incinerator"; September 6, 1985, "Garbage Plant in Brooklyn Protested"; January 7, 1987, "State Recommends Plan to Reduce Solid Wastes"; November 15, 1987, "Brooklyn Refuse Plan Raises Broad Concerns."
Nyhart, J.D., and Milton M. Carrow. 1983. *Law and Science in Collaboration*. Lexington, MA: Lexington Books.
O'Connor, James. 1973. *The Fiscal Crisis of the State*. New York: St. Martin's Press.
Ozawa, Connie P., and Lawrence E. Susskind. 1985. "Mediating Science-Intensive Policy Disputes," *Journal of Policy Analysis and Management*. 5(1): 23-39.
Polanyi, Michael. 1972. "The Republic of Science: Its Political and Economic Theory," *Minerva*. 1: 54-73.
Price, Don K. 1965. *The Scientific Estate*. Cambridge, MA: The Belknap Press of Harvard University Press.
Primack, Joel, and Frank Von Hippel. 1974. *Advice and Dissent: Scientists in the Political Arena*. New York: New American Library.
Raloff, Janet. 1985. "Dioxin: Is Everyone Contaminated?" *Science News*. 128: 26-29.
Reisel, Daniel. 1985. "Negotiation and Mediation of Environmental Disputes," *Ohio State Journal on Dispute Resolution*. 1(1): 99-111.

Rushefsky, Mark. 1984. "Institutional Mechanisms for Resolving Risk Controversies," in Susan G. Hadden, ed. *Risk Analysis, Institutions, and Public Policy*. New York: Associated Faculty Press.

———. 1986. *Making Cancer Policy*. Albany, NY: State University of New York Press.

Schattschneider, E.E. 1975. *The Semi-Sovereign People*. New York: Holt, Reinhold & Winston.

Sclove, Richard. 1982. "Decision-making in a Democracy," *Bulletin of the Atomic Scientists*. 38(5): 44–49.

Selznick, Philip. 1949. *TVA and the Grass Roots*. Berkeley and Los Angeles: University of California Press.

Simkin, William. 1971. *Mediation and the Dynamics of Collective Bargaining*. Washington, D.C.: Bureau of National Affairs.

Singer, Linda. 1990. *Settling Disputes*. Boulder, CO: Westview Press.

South Terminal Corporation v. EPA. 504 F.2d 646 (1st Cir. 1974).

Steisel, Norman, New York City Sanitation Commissioner. 1985. "A Major Step Toward Solving New York City's Waste Disposal Problem: Statements in Support of the Proposed Brooklyn Navy Yard Waste-to-Energy Project," testimony before the New York City Board of Estimate. August 15, 1985.

Stewart, Richard B., and James E. Krier. 1978. *Environmental Law and Policy: Readings, Materials and Notes* (2nd ed.). Indianapolis: Bobbs-Merrill Co.

Susskind, Lawrence, and Jeffrey Cruikshank. 1987. *Breaking the Impasse*. New York: Basic Books.

Susskind, Lawrence, and Louise Dunlap. 1981. "The Importance of Non-Objective Judgments in Environmental Impact Assessment," *Environmental Impact Assessment Review*. 2(4): 335–366.

Susskind, Lawrence, and Scott McCreary. 1985. "Techniques for ResolvingCoastal Resource Management Disputes Through Negotiation," *APA Journal*. (Summer): 365–374.

Susskind, Lawrence, and Gerard McMahon. 1985. "The Theory and Practice of Negotiated Rulemaking," *Yale Journal on Regulation*. 3(1): 133–165.

Susskind, Lawrence, and Connie Ozawa. 1983. "Mediated Negotiation in the Public Sector," *American Behavioral Scientist*. 27(2): 255–279.

United States v. Michigan. 1980. 653f.2nd 277, (6th Cir. 1980).

United States v. Michigan. 1985. File No. M26–73CA (W.D. Mich. Apr. 10, 1985) (Consent Order).

United States Environmental Protection Agency. 1985(a). Internal memorandum from Acting Assistant Administrator for Air and Radiation (ANR–443), c. July 3, 1985.

———. 1985(b). Internal memorandum. August 16, 1985.

———. 1986. Meeting notes on Regulatory Negotiation for the Woodstove NSPS (New Source Performance Standards). March 20–21, April 17–18, May 19–20, June 11–12, July 16–18, August 20–21, 1986. Unpublished.

Wall, James A., and Dale E. Rude. 1985. "Judicial Mediation: Techniques, Strategies, and Situational Effects," *Journal of Social Issues*. 41(2): 47–63.

The Wall Street Journal, January 13, 1986, "Group's Influence on U.S. Environmental Laws, Policies Earns It a Reputation as a Shadow EPA."

Wanderstock, Helen. 1984. "Westway," in Dorothy Nelkin, ed. *Controversy: Politics of Technical Decisions*. Beverly Hills: Sage Publications.
Weinberg, Alan. 1972. "Science and Trans-science," *Minerva*. 10: 209–22.
Wenner, Lettie M. 1982. *The Environmental Decade in Court*. Bloomington, IN: Indiana University Press.
West, William F. 1985. *Administrative Rulemaking: Politics and Processes*. Westport, CT: Greenwood Press.
Wildavsky, Aaron. 1979. *Speaking Truth to Power*. New York: Basic Books.
Wilson, James Q. 1980. *The Politics of Regulation*. New York: Basic Books.
Wood, Robert C. 1964. "Scientists and Politics: The Rise of a Apolitical Elite," in Robert Gilpin and Christopher Wright, eds. *Scientists and National Policy-Making*. New York: Columbia University Press.

Index

Abrams, Nancy Ellen, 34
Accountability in decision making, 4–5
Administrative decision making, 13, 19–22, 28, 30
Administrative Procedures Act (APA), 4
Agenda-setting, 80–82, 96, 102(nn 1, 2)
Albury, Randall, 46
Alternative solutions, 58–59, 84–85, 88–89, 97
American Medical Association, 2, 12(n1)
Anti-smoking campaign. *See* Cigarette smoking controversy
APA. *See* Administrative Procedures Act
Ashford, Nicholas A., 39

Bacon, Francis, 6–7
Bacow, Lawrence, 18, 47, 50
Barry, Donald B., 4
BATNA. *See* Best alternative to a negotiated settlement
Ben-David, Joseph, 7, 46
Berry, R. Stephen, 34
Best alternative to a negotiated settlement (BATNA), 116, 124, 126(n2)
Boffey, Philip, 40
Brickman, Ronald, 9
Brooklyn Navy Yard project. *See* New York City waste disposal case
Brooks, Harvey, 7, 35, 47, 48
Brownstein, M., 62
Burger, Edward J., 8

CAC. *See* Citizen advisory committees

Carrow, Milton M., 34
Cigarette smoking controversy, 3, 9, 13, 38
  manipulative communications in, 36
  political interests in, 11
  problem formulation in, 83
  scientific disagreement in, 1–2, 48
Cigler, Allan J., 10
Citizen advisory committees (CAC), 18, 19, 31–32, 43(n15)
Clean Air Act, 4, 12(n4), 20, 84
Cobb, Roger W., 80, 81
Commoner, Barry, 10, 52, 57, 58, 59
Communications
  in consensus-based decision making, 63, 73
  in conventional decision making, 9, 34–36, 43(n16), 48–49
Community groups. *See* Policy stakeholders
Consensus-based decision making, 45, 102
  agenda-setting in, 80–82, 96
  alternative solutions in, 84–85, 97
  decision choice in, 85–87
  Michigan fishing case, 66–72, 75–76, 110
  new philosophy of science in, 46–47, 76(n1)
  New York City waste disposal case, 51–60, 73, 75, 88–89, 102(n5), 110, 111
  political interests in, 57–58, 65–66, 73–74, 110–112, 125
  power dynamics in, 87–102
  problem formulation in, 82–84, 96–97

139

role of scientist in, 74, 116, 120-122
and scientific disagreement, 46-50, 51-60, 70-72, 73-74, 75
viability of, 112-122, 123-126
wood stove emissions case, 60-66, 73, 74, 75, 89-92, 107, 110
Constructivist philosophy. *See* New philosophy of science
Consumer groups. *See* Policy stakeholders
Consumer Protection and Safety Act (CPSA), 4
Conventional decision making
administrative, 13, 19-22, 28, 30
costs of, 106
distortion of political concerns in, 33, 37-39
effects of consensus-based decision making on, 124-125
by elected officials, 13, 15-19, 28
judicial, 13, 22-29, 30-31, 42(n8)
power dynamics in, 106
role of scientist in, 39-41, 74, 121
scientific disagreement in, 1-3, 27-28, 32, 33-36, 43(n13)
Cormick, Gerald W., 50
Cost-benefit analysis, 5, 11
Council for Tobacco Research-U.S.A., 1, 2
Courts. *See* Judicial decision making; *specific cases*
CPSA. *See* Consumer Protection and Safety Act
Crandall, Robert W., 8
Cruikshank, Jeffrey, 34, 41, 126

Decision choice, 85-87, 97, 102(n5)
Delay, costs and benefits of, 13-15, 41-42, 125
Dickson, David, 8, 40
Dioxins. *See* New York City waste disposal controversy
Doherty, Robert, 66, 86
Douglas, Mary, 9
Dunlap, Louise, 47

EIS. *See* Environmental Impact Statement
Elder, Charles D., 80, 81
Elected officials, decision making by, 13, 15-19, 28
Enslen, Judge Richard, 27, 70
Environmental groups. *See* Policy stakeholders
Environmental Impact Statement (EIS), 3, 17, 18
Environmental Protection Agency (EPA), 34, 35, 39-40, 41
on dioxins, 18, 43(n13)
expert consultation by, 29, 30
See also Gasoline lead additive controversy; Wood stove emissions case
EPA. *See* Environmental Protection Agency
Error, 32, 49, 62
Ethyl Corporation v. EPA. *See* Gasoline lead additive controversy
Executive Order 12991, 64
Expert consultation, 29-30, 32, 35, 37, 40
in consensus-based decision making, 63-64, 73

Federal Water Pollution Control Act, 12(n4)
Fischer, Carl William, 5
Freedman, James O., 10
Freedom of Information Act, 5
Fritschler, A. Lee, 1, 2

Gasoline lead additive controversy, 2-3, 9, 11, 23, 40, 41
Great Lakes fishing case. *See* Michigan fishing case
Greenfield, Liah, 8
Gusfield, Joseph, 35, 83, 84

Hart, Fred C. *See* Hart report
Harter, Philip J., 60
Hart report, 19, 52, 53, 54, 55, 111
Hiskes, Anne L., 6

Index

Hiskes, Richard P., 6
Hubbard, Ruth, 47

Intervenor, 50, 57, 63, 76(n3)

Johnson, Lyndon B., 10
Judicial decision making, 13, 22-29, 30-31, 42(n8)

Kantrowitz, Arthur, 32
Knaster, Alana, 50
Knelman, Fred H., 10
Knorr-Cetina, Karin D., 47
Konkel, R. Steven, 51
Krier, James E., 10
Kuhn, Thomas, 46, 47

Lakoff, Sanford A., 4, 6, 7
Lapp, Ralph E., 7
Latour, Bruno, 47
Lave, Lester B., 8
Legislation, 4-5, 85. *See also specific legislation*
Levanthal, Harold, 23
Little, Timothy G., 31
Lobbying, 20-21, 42(nn 6, 7)
Logical positivist empiricism, 6-8, 11-12, 32, 40, 41, 46. *See also* Conventional decision making
Logrolling, 62
Longino, Helen, 47
Loomis, Burdett A., 10
Lowe, Theodore, 4

McCarthy, Jane, 34
McCreary, Scott, 50
McGovern, Francis, 67-68, 70-72, 93, 94, 95
McMahon, Gerard, 22
Majone, Giandomenico, 8
Marcus, Alfred A., 9, 62
Marine Protection Research Sanctuaries Act, 1972, 12(n4)
Mazur, Allan, 35, 36, 47
Mediator. *See* Intervenor
Melnick, R. Shep, 9

Merryman, Walter, 2
Michigan fishing case, 24, 28-29, 77(n17), 79, 125
 consensus-based decision making in, 66-72, 75-76, 110
 power dynamics in, 93-96, 98
Mulkay, Michael, 46
Mullins, Nicholas, 4

NAS. *See* National Academy of Sciences
National Academy of Sciences (NAS), 30, 40
National Environmental Policy Act (NEPA), 3-4, 17, 42(n1), 85
Nelkin, Dorothy, 8, 9
NEPA. *See* National Environmental Policy Act
New philosophy of science, 46-47, 76(n1)
New York City waste disposal case, 13, 15-19, 28, 29, 31, 42(nn 2, 3), 43(n13)
 agenda-setting in, 81-82
 alternative solutions in, 58-59, 84-85, 88-89
 communications in, 35
 consensus-based decision making in, 51-60, 73, 75, 88-89, 102(n5), 110, 111
 decision choice in, 86, 97, 102(n5)
 delayed decision in, 41
 political interests in, 37-38, 106
 problem formulation in, 82-83, 84, 96-97
 scientific disagreement in, 18-19, 51-60, 75
NIMBY. *See* Not-in-my-backyard (NIMBY) concerns
Noise Control Act, 1972, 12(n4)
Not-in-my-backyard (NIMBY) concerns, 18, 59
NRDC v. EPA. *See* Wood stove emissions case
Nyhart, J. D., 34

Occupational Health and Safety Act (OSHA), 4
Occupational Health and Safety Administration (OSHA), 30
O'Connor, James, 10
Office of Management and Budget, 64
Office of Technology Assessment (OTA), 5
OSHA. *See* Occupational Health and Safety Act; Occupational Health and Safety Administration
OTA. *See* Office of Technology Assessment

Philosophies of science. *See* Logical positivist empiricism; New philosophy of science
Polanyi, Michael, 7
Policy dialogue, 16, 56–60, 88–89, 96–97, 102(n5), 110
Policy stakeholders, 10, 28–29, 43(n14)
  benefits of consensus-based decision making for, 117–120, 123–124
  and communications, 34, 36
  and delays in decision making, 13–15, 125
  empowerment of, 88–93, 96–97, 98–101, 102(n5), 117–118, 123
  expectations of rights by, 10
  hardening of positions, 38
  lobbying by, 20–21
  non-negotiable demands, 125–126
  political interests of, 11, 37–39, 106
  support for research, 10–11, 12, 13
  varying resources of, 12, 21
  See also Political interests; *specific cases*
Political interests, 11, 106
  agenda-setting, 80–81
  in consensus-based decision making, 57–58, 65–66, 73–74, 110–112, 125
  distortion of, 33, 37–39, 40, 59–60
  political horsetrading, 86
  and problem formulation, 82–84
  vs. science as neutral, 8, 110–111
  scientific information as tool for, 1–4, 8–9, 33–34, 69–70, 76, 122

  See also Scientific disagreement
Pollack, Michael, 8
Power dynamics, 79, 87, 93–96, 106
  empowerment of policy stakeholders, 88–93, 96–97, 98–101, 102(n5), 117–118, 123
President's Science Advisory Committee, 5
Price, Don K., 7
Primack, Joel, 11
Problem formulation, 82–84, 96–97
Public credibility, 19, 40, 116–117, 121
Public participation in policy making, 10, 17. *See also* Policy stakeholders

Rabinowitz, Francine, 71
Raloff, Janet, 18
Regulatory negotiations. *See* Wood stove emissions case
Reisel, Daniel, 41
Risk-benefit analysis, 5
Roosevelt, Franklin D., 4

Safe Drinking Water Act, 1974, 12(n4)
Schattschneider, E. E., 38
Scientific disagreement
  consensus-based approaches to, 46–50, 51–60, 70–72, 73–74, 75
  conventional approaches to, 1–3, 18–19, 27–28, 32, 33–36, 43(n13)
  and expert consultation, 29, 32, 37, 40
  inevitability of, 12, 46–47, 105–106, 110
  See also Political interests; Scientific information
Scientific information
  conventional methods of handling, 28–41, 76
  as mechanism of accountability, 4–5
  as neutral, 6–8, 11–12, 32, 40, 46
  packaging of, 36, 48–49
  as political weapon, 1–4, 8–9, 33–34, 69–70, 76, 122
  as source of authority, 5–8, 84
  See also Scientific disagreement

Index

Scientist, role of, 39–41, 74, 116, 120–122. *See also* Expert consultation; Scientific disagreement; Scientific information
Selznick, Philip, 31
Singer, Linda, 119
South Terminal Corporation v. EPA, 23–24
Special masters, 30–31, 35, 67–68, 70–72, 76
Steisel, Norman, 16, 18
Stewart, Richard B., 10
Straus, Don, 51
Susskind, Lawrence, 22, 34, 41, 47, 50, 126

Task forces, 30
Technological advances, 9–10
Tobacco Industry Research Committee. *See* Council for Tobacco Research-U.S.A.
Tobacco Institute, Inc., 2, 9, 12(n2), 36
Toxic Substances Control Act (TSCA), 4
TSCA. *See* Toxic Substances Control Act

United States v. Michigan, 24

Von Hippel, Frank, 11

Wanderstock, Helen, 3
Weinberg, Alan, 46
Wessel, Milton R., 49
West, William F., 4
West Side Highway (New York City), 3–4, 13, 19
Westway Project. *See* West Side Highway (New York City)
Wheeler, Michael, 50
Whitcomb, Howard R., 4
Wildavsky, Aaron, 9, 82
Wilson, James Q., 11
Wood, Robert D., 7
Wood stove emissions case, 19–22, 28, 41, 42, 102(n5)
  agenda-setting in, 82, 96
  alternative solutions in, 85, 97
  consensus-based decision making in, 60–66, 73, 74, 75, 89–92, 107, 110
  decision choice in, 86–87, 97
  power dynamics in, 89–92
  problem formulation in, 84